THE DEFENCE OF THE
HOLY HESYCHASTS

PRAXIS

Saint Gregory Palamas

TRIADS IN DEFENCE OF THE HOLY HESYCHASTS

VOLUME I

Translated by Robin Amis
- Director of Praxis Research Institute, author of
A Different Christianity, published by
State University of New York Press, 1995.

Historical Introduction by David Vermette.
Production assisted by The Early Christian Translation Fund,
UK Registered Charity No. 1088733

PRAXIS

VOLUME I

THE FIRST TRIAD

We would like to acknowledge the excellent critical
edition of John Meyendorff's French translation from the
Greek, as well as Nicholas Gendle's English translation
of selections from the Triads.

PRAXIS INSTITUTE PRESS
A DIVISION OF PRAXIS RESEARCH INSTITUTE, INC.
A NON-PROFIT CORPORATION REGISTERED IN THE STATE OF
MASSACHUSETTS, REG.NO. 043-110-773
Three Barns, Aish Lane, South Brent, Devon. TQ10 9JF UK
- and at: 2931 W. Belmont Ave. Chicago, IL 60618 USA

Printed in Great Britain by
Booksprint, Wellington, Somerset

British Library cataloguing-in-publication data:
St, Gregory Palamas
'Volume 1 - THE FIRST TRIAD'

British Library Cataloguing-in-Publication Data:
A catalogue record for this book is available
from the British Library.

ISBN 1-872292-15-1

ACKNOWLEDGEMENTS

We acknowledge our gratitude to the many people who have helped us complete this translation and discover in the English language the unique Christian philosophy of this late Byzantine saint. In particular we wish to recognise the assistance of David Vermette, Dr. Seymour Simmons, of Alex Kosmatopoulos, Greek poet and translator of Mallory's *Morte d'Arthur* into Greek, as well as certain monks of the Athonite monastery of Osiou Gregoriou, particularly Father Damianos and Father Artemius. Finally I must acknowledge the help of my wife, Lillian Amis, both for her tolerance of my long hours of silence devoted to this task, and for not being afraid to comment openly on the text wherever it was necessary.

Robin Amis

O Star of Orthodoxy, support of the Church,
and its teacher,
O comeliness of ascetics,
and incontestable champion of those who speak of theology,
Gregory wonder-worker,
the pride of Thessalonica and preacher of grace,
pray without ceasing for the salvation of our souls.

- Greek Orthodox Troparion to Saint Gregory Palamas   -

CONTENTS

The cover painting is an icon of St. Gregory Palamas by Lillian Delevoryas, wife of Robin Amis, translator of this volume of the Triads. Lillian, an American artist of Greek ancestry, came to iconograhy later in life, bringing to it the skills acquired by years as a renowned flower painter, giving her a unique way of expressing this ancient tradition in our times.

Recently, his Eminence, Archbishop Gregorios of Thyateira and Great Britain, commended her art as 'combining age-old spirituality with a modern idiom and inspiration, taken from the world of nature.'

CONTENTS

. . . . Sister . . . .

. . . .

TRIADS IN DEFENCE OF THE HOLY HESYCHASTS

INTRODUCTION

THE FIRST TRIAD

TRANSLATOR'S INTRODUCTION

Saint Gregory Palamas was a monk, a scholar, a bishop, and a figure of some historical importance. He was also a hesychast, a practitioner of the hesychastic inner stillness taught by the early fathers of the church as a way of opening the mind to God. In those days, the mainstream of Christian spirituality was still centred around the ascetic exercises first recommended by Saint Paul.[1] For the hesychasts, many of them living away from people or in monastic communities, these exercises were taken as a complete way of life - a Christian equivalent of the practices of monks and hermits in eastern faiths.

By the fourth century, the Christian use of the word hesychia was clearly and precisely defined, as when it was used: *'to describe the state of inner rest and silence which victory over the passions gained for a monk, and so allowed him to proceed to contemplation.'*[2] The term was used by Gregory of Nyssa in his *'Life of Moses,'* which - in addition to Gregory Palamas' *Triads* - gives one of the best definitions of the contemplative mysticism of Nyssa's slightly earlier time. This was one of the stages through which the teaching of the church was developed further to correct a growing loss of understanding of the original New Testament teaching, a loss which still continues today.

It was in these elaborations of the original Christian teaching that differences between the inner and outer churches, the ascetic and the purely liturgical forms of Christianity, first began to become visible. Saint Gregory Palamas' *Triads* played - and continue to play - an important part in this.

As far as I know, this translation of Palamas' *Triads* is the first complete translation into English undertaken. It is certainly different in emphasis from what I have found. Its source is found in the same texts as Nicholas Gendle's translation in the Classics of Western Spirituality series.[3] It has attempted to address a question previously addressed in the earlier version - that of the existence in the same text of detailed spiritual teaching alongside what appeared to Meyendorff, the translator of the book into French and advisor on the previous English translation, to be polemical.

Studied in this way, the book itself is then found to reveal unexpected characteristics of the culture which gave it birth. An understanding of these characteristics as they are understood in practice in the same geographical region to this day, on Mount Athos in particular, transforms and clarifies the meaning of the translated text. In its light, much of what has been seen as based on a polemical attitude is revealed as a genuine defence of the methods of spirituality which formed the basic motif - the 'scientific discipline' - of the hesychastic culture of the eastern churches. What remains polemical is shown in a different light by this same fact. It can now be clearly seen as a genuine treatise on knowledge and truth from the viewpoint of that different culture, and we can see that the polemical element serves, in a way commonly used by authors of that time, as a mask intended to cover some of their deeper teachings in order to avoid causing confusion.

In this translation, certain words of psychological meaning have been left in the original Greek, particularly *nous* and *psyche*, which in our times are both found to be translated in many very different ways, some of these differences being reflected in the Meyendorff translation. Wherever possible throughout this new translation the Greek words are translated by a single English word.

In essence, the unexpected conclusion from the translation of this book was that over the past thousand years or so, alongside the advance of science and technology, there had been a general deterioration in our deeper understanding of ourselves and the world, a deterioration in which the vast majority of people had begun to think of things not as they can be understood, but simply as they appear at a cursory glance, taken without intervening thought. As I hope to show later in a separate book, not only did these factors suggest that there has been a change which has been in some way harmful to our humanity, but they gave pointers to ways in which this damage might be undone.

This possibility of a cure is one of the reasons for raising this question in such a book as this. Later I shall explain the way in which these observations link to the special way this translation approaches the ideas of *nous* and *psyche*. Translating these words in the way used here provides a number of clues to the deeper meaning of the text, and I am already convinced that this deeper meaning has the most practical significance.

ANOTHER WAY OF KNOWING

It is well-known that Palamas' theology, particularly as expressed in the polemical side of the Triads, was closely involved with the struggle against the rationalist thought that had already begun to change the doctrine of the Western churches during his lifetime. This rationalism of his time was associated with a reawakening of certain elements of pre-Christian philosophical thought, known by Palamas, as sometimes known today, by the name of 'Hellenistic thinking,' an approach that was closely allied to the stream of thought which has since then led to massive changes in the thinking of the Western churches. It also seems that it was this rationalist divergence from Christ's original teaching which in our time has led to the decline of the Christian religion in the West. During this change, a teaching about a God Who is repeatedly described as inaccessible to the senses and inexplicable to reason becomes inexplicably rationalised and 'made sensible.'

It was Palamas, in his writings, who probably best defined the flaws in this belief by defining a different way in which God can be known. His approach to this question is neither based on sensory observation nor intellectual analysis, although it does require an intellectual understanding that there can exist *another way of knowing,* different from that of modern scientific and rationalistic thought. But his answer has until now been little understood in the West. So far is this concept from modern thought, that it is only those who have sufficient experience of the effective spiritual practices of that time who will see the truth of Palamas' argument. From that, they may then come to understand that reason won the day in those troubled times - at least from the point of view of the hesychastic communities of Orthodox Christianity. As a direct result of this, the spirituality of the West today is often no more than a diluted form of what once existed in the Eastern church.

This failure of knowledge was not only a failure to clarify belief: it was also a failure of European thought - from Palamas' time until now - to explain certain elements of human inner experience. Certainly, its outcome has now shaped life in the West for more than seven hundred years. The upshot of all this is that Palamas and his Triads tell us a great deal about the history of the church around seven hundred years ago, when its early success finally came to an end. In a very real sense, Palamas' text is or was actually a part of that history; it played a part in the events surrounding the change of that time. It contains much information about that period, so that to understand its historical significance gives it greater value. More, the book is the summation, the last line of defence, and at the same time the encapsulation of the first millennium Christian culture ... the culture which was the *arche*, the origin from which, more than any other single society, our modern Civilisation sprang.

This very text, translated on the following pages, uniquely defines the boundaries-in-time of that culture, for the author tells us how and almost exactly when it began, and how and exactly when - to within five years or so, an acceptable accuracy over seven-hundred years - it began to end. More recent researches into the questions it has raised have also helped us to understand its significance; the different concept of religion that existed in that time; the reality of its outcome; the intelligence of its proponents. One set of clues was found by taking account of the understanding that just as language shapes thought, so the outer and inner forces which shape our life also shape our language. In this way the language of Hesychast monks like Saint Gregory Palamas was shaped by lives driven by the search for God and the striving for repentance. Their language distinguished theological ideas, philosophical criteria, and psychological states - each of these taken to a fine point which, when we first hear of them, seem to show them as little different from one another and thus of little importance.

If we study these ideas for the time they deserve, their meaning can begin to grow on us, their importance become apparent. In the first of the three volumes of Palamas' *Triads*, for long famous in the Eastern church, this happens not just in one subject that is now - in our era of specialisation - regarded as a separate discipline, but in many different fields. In many of those fields this book is important.

* It is important to the churches, because it gives a way of answering questions about the causes of the loss of faith in our times.

* It is psychologically important in many ways, therapeutic as well as theoretical, particularly because it points to ways once known of integration, or as Jung would call it, individuation, of the human psyche.

* It is philosophically important, because it provides a number of answers that have been lost for many centuries, including 'new' or long-lost answers to some of the classical questions of philosophy.

* And, as we will slowly come to realise, for us today, it is historically and socially important for all these reasons.

The fact that language shapes thought underlies the method which, in this translation, systematically translates key words in a way that will reveal our understanding of how Palamas and the hesychasts of his time once thought. This is important because, in the Western translations of this work that have been available until now, not only *nous,* but certain other Greek words, have been given multiple meanings varying according to the context. There were obviously good reasons for some of these variations: for example, they would fit more easily into modern thought. Yet in fact some of them seem to produce certain confusions in the reader. As we worked on this text, it began to appear that the confusions themselves, once understood, were showing us one of the most important conclusions to be drawn from the text. They revealed how different are the conclusions drawn by our contemporary thought from that of the first Christian millennium, giving glimpses of a fundamental divergence between two very different ways of seeing the world. Contrasting these two world-views showed that they influenced perception itself, presenting the world to the psyche in two ways that appeared remarkably different one from the other.

Under the influence of the normal contemporary Western world-view, the way things appear to the senses is taken as the nature of those things in themselves. This means that any difference in how they appear to us appears, tautologously, as a difference in their nature. That is to say that different appearances of one thing are mistakenly seen as if they were different things, subject to different laws, in direct contradiction to the millennia-old philosophical understanding that apparent differences are not real, they are only apparent differences caused when the same thing is seen in different ways. Philosophical insights of this kind, which helped to shape our civilisation in the past, have little influence over people today. They count for little in a celebrity culture.

From the psychological viewpoint, another remarkable example of the effects of the shift in meaning of a word from its single sense as referring to a single object, to explaining its varied sensory appearances by using different words for different appearances. One example is a most important word from classical Greek, the linguistic root of our understanding of psychology: *psyche*. Among the varied translations of this word psyche are some that are among the most important concepts in contemporary thought. One problem is that the translations of psyche overlap with those of other words - many of them found in the *Triads* - *nous*, for instance, and *dianoia*. In the French translation of Palamas' *Triads*, both psyche and nous are at different times translated by *esprit*. In a previous English translation the same principle has been applied, so that both are given as *mind*. As well as 'mind,' there are several other English words that are also used to render the Greek psyche. Life is one, and soul, one of the most imprecise terms in the English language, is another. As I shall show later, in our present age, there is a divergence between what is understood by one of these different meanings and what is understood by another. We do not always think of them as the same thing. For example:

* *Soul:* Sometimes thought to be something within us that departs at death, and is said in our theology to be the subject of 'salvation.'

* *Psyche:* The subject of our psychology.

* *Life:* The life-processes that begin at birth and end at death.

* *Mind:* The mental factor that is the concern of philosophical questions such as the famous 'mind-brain' problem.

The divergence between these different meanings of a single word lies like a warning-flag exactly on the primary or most important fault-line that divides our fragmented Western civilisation, at just the place where in-depth investigation would be recommended if someone wished to understand and perhaps heal that fragmentation. This is not accidental. Each of these different appearances that represent the psyche underlies significant misunderstandings about human nature; misunderstandings which have helped to shape modern life. All relate to a question that was recurrent in philosophy even before the original Greek awakening. Christian doctrine, and in the same way ancient teachings such as the Vedas, are all subject to a particular type of decay. Over the centuries, as they have become diffused, they then become fragmented, and their doctrines become increasingly dualistic, materialistic, and anthropocentric.

The inescapable conclusion of all this is that to understand this word psyche, in particular, we have to think about all of this very carefully. So first we will further develop three of the most important meanings of the word:

1. **Psyche** consists primarily of thoughts, feelings, memories, impulses and so on which arise within us and pass through the field of our attention. We experience these things inside ourselves and never outside. Some modern thinkers, like David Bohm, call all of this 'thought.' Mind is sometimes taken as synonymous with psyche, sometimes, in Cartesian terms, as one side of the 'mind-body' problem of contemporary philosophy.

2. **Soul** is spoken about in theory, in translations of doctrine, and in myth, but I have never met anybody who was entirely sure in what way it was experienced... except as we experience the psyche.

3. **Life** exists, tautologously, in every living creature or, in a slightly different way, in plants. Crystals grow too, but we may find it difficult to be sure that they are alive. The first and most obvious sign by which we recognise life is in movement, including speech. But people also seem to recognise it in the smaller movements that exist out of our sight within living creatures: in digestion; the circulation of the blood and the movement of other fluids; in the tensing of muscles; in whatever nervous activity is perceptible to us.

There are two different lessons in these observations. The first is that, seen in different ways, one thing can look like things that are entirely different. What it seems to be - how it appears - depends entirely on the way we perceive it. The interesting thing is that, under different circumstances, one or another of those three appearances seems to be 'obvious' or 'intuitive.'

10

The second lesson relates specifically to the understanding of the psyche. Each different word for it, in representing a different appearance, represents a different way in which the concept of psyche can be understood, and in our times, at least, these different viewpoints on the one thing known as the psyche lead to conflicting ways of understanding and thinking about it - ways that cannot all be true. A little thought will show that some of these conflicting viewpoints can only be totally misleading.

One result is that different disciplines think about the same object in different ways. Modern theology thinks about soul, often meaning psyche, in a particular way. Modern psychology thinks about psyche as mind or as certain processes of mind. Biology thinks of life, and translates the Greek concepts of psyche as life, more in a way linked to chemistry. Considered on the basis of how it is seen by the senses, each of the three thus seems to be entirely different from the other two.

But if we can manage to remember and keep in mind that all these three appearances are in essence just one thing, then we will find that we can begin to understand it in a different and more complete way.

In fact, each different meaning of the word represents a different 'appearance' - but each is a different appearance of the same 'reality.'

THE INNER EYE, OR NOUS

Underlying this difference in meaning is the fact that it can be seen as providing evidence of different states of mind. The division in the appearance of the psyche is in part the product of a division between alternative ways in which we may become aware of the psyche. In particular there is one major divergence revealed in how we conceive of the psyche: we see it as different and differing fragments, or we see it as a unity, and this difference occurs in part because both situations occur in the psyche at different times, depending on the state of that part of the psyche which the Greeks called the *nous*.

The action of the human nous is found in attention - the Greek word for attention is also nous, the one word describes the thing and

11

its activity. Attention is also linked to awareness and recognition, and the unity of the nous underlies both inner and outer perception. But because the outer is obvious, the inner is often ignored. Thus the division of meanings is rooted in a division in our perceptions. Such *apparent* divisions do not exist in the substance of what is perceived, but arise only in that which perceives. Differences in perception stem from different ways of perceiving something, not from essential differences in what is perceived. A nous when its attention is lost in the activities of the nous, is fragmented, its awareness divided, and this is the root of division itself.

All these three - life, soul, and psyche, then - are apparent divisions in this sense, but their different appearances are based on real differences in the way we perceive the one thing which is the psyche.

In the case of nous, the confusion created by the existence of multiple appearances of a single thing has once again led to difficulties in translating this Greek word. *Nous* is now most often translated not as the knowing core of reason, but as a word now understood to refer only to the everyday thoughts, a term which describes its coinage but not its value: its form but not its full meaning. In some way, this difference in appearance represents a breakdown, a narrowing, in our ability to understand - not only a limitation in our ability to understand Palamas' book, but also in our ability to understand experience. Further enquiry suggests that this was evidence of a conceptual fragmentation symptomatic of a widespread general deterioration in the use of the human mind, and even to suggest certain reasons for this deterioration. It appears more than possible that modern problems such as ADD, (Attention Deficit Disorder,) might directly result from this. In the Greek of Palamas' time, attention is an action of the nous.

In fact nous, as described by Palamas and the fathers who had gone before him, is not just 'psyche,' but the highest part of psyche: *'the eye of the psyche,'* the long-lost ruling 'inmost-heart' of the human psyche. It is through the actions of the nous, and of grace acting through that nous, that, as St. Maximos says: *"Man remains wholly man in psyche and body, and through grace becomes wholly God in psyche and body."*

With nous, as with psyche, the difference between the way it appears from different viewpoints leads to our concluding wrongly that these different aspects originate from different objects, since the different names, representing different appearances, seem to belong to what are actually different things. To think about different appearances of a single thing as if they represented different things behaving in entirely different ways: what is this, if not a serious confusion in our thinking?

HESYCHIAH: THE STILLNESS THAT KNOWS GOD

The Christian use of the word hesychia was first defined in the fourth century, and in Gregory of Nyssa's *'Life of Moses'* it was used to help define the contemplative mysticism of the time. This was one of the stages during which the teaching of the church was developed further to correct for growing divergence from the original stream of the New Testament teaching. It was in these elaborations of the original Christian teaching that the distinction between inner and outer, the ascetic and the purely liturgical forms of Christianity, first began to become visible. (It should be noted here that the ascetic forms almost always include the liturgical aspect of the faith, although the opposite is not true.)

Palamas' writings, particularly the *Triads*, relate to a further elaboration that became necessary for the same reasons, so that his theology is closely involved with the struggle against the rationalist thought which since then has led to massive changes in the Western churches. It is those changes – that divergence from Christ's original teaching – which has led to the decline of the Christian religion in the Western churches.

The importance of this relates to the idea that has been expressed simplistically in the saying that: *"It is said that Christianity has been tried and failed. In fact it has never failed, because it has never been properly tried."* Correctly understood, Palamas' writings give the lie to this saying, showing that Christianity was originally successful, but the complete teaching of the successful form never reached the West except to very small groups of people. Yet today it still survives, hidden within the Eastern churches. The truth is that Christianity has been repeatedly tried and has repeatedly succeeded on a small scale, but that is is failed to spread from those successive small beginnings without being so distorted that it becomes almost ineffective.

TWO KINDS OF THINKING

In Part One of this First Volume of his *Triads*, Palamas begins by defining the fine distinctions between the two kinds of wisdom described by Saint Paul: the Wisdom of the World, and the Wisdom of God. When we first begin to study this, it seems needlessly complex, but once it is fully understood, it comes to life and then seems entirely meaningful. As we study it, we find that we have also drawn in the outline of an answer to one as-yet unanswered contemporary question: the proper relation of science and religion as two different forms of knowledge obtained in different ways and serving two quite different purposes. The link with the nous lies in the fact that one of these forms of wisdom is intellectual and rational. One seems to glimpse ways in which past mistranslations of nous have been responsible for the over-emphasis on this intellectual aspect. *"Therefore the light of Christ in us is … the foundation of hesychast spirituality. The contrast between knowledge coming from outside – a human and purely symbolic knowledge – and 'noetic' knowledge coming from within, is found already in Pseudo-Dionysius: it is not from without that God moves them towards the divine, but in a noetic way, by illuminating them from within with the most divine will by means of a pure and immaterial light."* [4] The confusion of intellectual and sensory sources of knowledge with 'noetic' knowledge coming from within explains the varied beliefs normal in and between the modern churches.

Noetic knowledge is not imagination, but true intuition, in the sense that it is the only form of intuition which tells true: knowledge whose source is subjective, but whose accuracy is best defined by the term objective. We can think of it, paradoxically, as 'inner objectivity.'

This discussion between the two kinds of knowledge and the two kinds of thinking that belong to them is largely found in Part One of the present translation. Its implications are developed in Part Two, when Palamas moves on to the question of what today is known as personal development. Both first and third parts hinge on the fact that in Palamas' time as in our own, people were forced to the belief that human reason, aided only by the senses and logic, was unable to know God directly. This disbelief in ability of human reason to know God leads, says Meyendorff, to two alternatives.[5] The evidence is either hearsay or experiential.

1. Hearsay evidence leads to dependence on scripture. This can seem to be 'mere hearsay' unless we have the second:

2. The experiential or experimental evidence is defined in the classic hesychast formula in which we know God, not directly and immediately, but as a result of certain of His actions which we can observe. The earliest full expression of this formula was probably in the *Triads*. *"...the supernatural union with the more than resplendant light ... is the sole source of sure theology."*[6]

Of course, this is a final reduction of the problem which often appears as no more than a massive oversimplification. There is the suggestion that God can be known Platonically, as an Archetype, an idea that is the origin of all ideas. Then there is the idea of knowing God in our own actions. Evangelist Billy Graham once admitted on television that he was not entirely sure how much he should do to help bring others to God, and what he should leave to the Lord. In Part Two of his *First Triad,* Palamas goes into the fine points of what should be left to God, not in the transformation of others, but in our own spiritualisation. In doing so, he provides a method remarkably like Yoga, but still entirely Christian in its ultimate dependence on grace, and if we investigate it fully we discover that the 'early fathers' of the church tended to fall into two camps: those who drew from ancient teachings and emphasised the importance of individual effort, and those who drew mostly on the gospel, and emphasised the undoubted pre-eminence of faith and grace.

Throughout the long history of the 'patristic era,' when the church was shaped by the most spiritual of its 'fathers,' one of these fathers would fill the role of reconciler, skilfully organising this knowledge so that the proper and living relationship between the two aspects became visible again. Not only was Palamas, as described by

Meyendorff, such a man, but his thought was particularly important as summing up the thinking of his kind and his era. *"Palamas,"* says Meyendorff, *"provided such a doctrine and a strict hierarchy of values. He did so by integrating the spiritual vocabulary derived from Evagrius and more recent psycho-physical methods of prayer with a harmonious conception of life in Jesus Christ. In this way he continued the work of the Fathers who, without avoiding those elements whose non-Christian origin could not be in doubt, adapted them – as reflections of natural mysticism - to the unique reality of the Christian mystery. It goes without saying that this adaptation inwardly modified the meaning of the terms employed, and put them in harmony with the Biblical teaching on man."*[7]

THE NOUS AS THE STILL AND SECRET SELF

Throughout all this, we find a common thread based on a psychological understanding almost entirely unknown in the West for near a thousand years. This thread is found simply by employing a consistent rendering of the classical Greek words 'nous' and 'psyche.' This is based on the judgement that at that time, and in that psychological context, each of these words was used as a technical term, having a single clear and precise meaning, that meaning defined by repeated experience. It is this 'full experiential meaning' which has long been forgotten, so that today these important words are translated in different ways at different times even within the context of the writings of Palamas, who is known to have been concerned to resolve differences in language used by different fathers, so that he will have used language with a professional precision. In other sources, nous is given as the French 'esprit,' normally translated in English as 'mind;' as Augustine's Latin 'intellectus,' which normally today comes into English as intellect, despite the fact that the modern use of this word 'intellect' is not remotely like the Platonic or Byzantine use of nous. It also appears in the Latin as 'ratio,' reason. The Cambridge Platonists spotted this latter, and in so doing uncovered in the Christian thought of the past, just that significance of the nous which we find in Palamas and other earlier fathers, a significance which gives the teachings of the fathers a 'holistic,' unitive meaning, nothing like the modern discursive intellect. It was then understood as the seat of inspiration and insight, the core of the attention, the spotlight of clarity. When 'magnetised' by love of God, it became the mysterious 'magnetic centre' of Russian hesychasm, a synonym for the Ark of bulrushes and later the Ark of the Covenant of Gregory of Nyssa's mythical Moses of the mind. It is found in mystical experience as the stillness beyond everyday life, the forgotten *Place of God* of the ancient mystics, with its 'sapphire pavement.

A silent psyche is a clear and open mind, but most of the time this part of the mind is not so silent.

Hesychasm was a way of learning to be inwardly silent.

HISTORICAL INTRODUCTION

by David Vermette

THE HESYCHAST CONTROVERSY AS HISTORY

Sometime in the early 1300s, Barlaam, a monk and scholar, came to the Byzantine capital to test his intellectual mettle against the learned minds of that city. Although he was Orthodox, and born Greek, Barlaam was a representative of the Western intellectualism of this period. At the same time, he was an opponent of the theology of Thomas Aquinas, and some historians have suggested that he was influenced by the 'nominalism' of such Western figures as the Oxford Franciscan William of Ockham, but this is largely conjecture.

In the 1330s, Barlaam was appointed by John Cantacuzenus, the 'Grand Domestic,' (an office akin to Prime Minister) and future Emperor of Byzantium, to a position at the great University of Constantinople. One of Barlaam's first intellectual opponents was the famous Byzantine historian and scholar Nicephoras Gregoras. Gregoras roundly defeated him in a public debate by revealing the limitations in Barlaam's knowledge of Aristotle. It was after this humiliation that Barlaam stirred up a controversy with the hesychast monks, thinking, perhaps, that they would provide an easier target. After spending some time in hesychast hermitages in Constantinople and near Thessaloniki, Barlaam began to make known his opposition to what he imagined to be the errors of the hesychast monks.

Whatever personal motives Barlaam may have had for his vigorous opposition to the hesychast teaching of the time, there is little doubt that he was genuinely shocked by what he learned from the

Eastern monks with whom he had contact, so great was the division in theology and practice between East and West even then. Because the heritage of the Desert Fathers had never been fully assimilated by the Western church, Barlaam found himself confronted by 'a different Christianity,' a Christianity that to someone of his training appeared heretical and even ridiculous.

Because of the differing concepts of knowledge between Eastern and Western churches, a difference which forms the main subject of the first Part of the First Triad now translated, Barlaam's opposition to the hesychasts fell mainly in the domain of what might be termed *theological epistemology.*

Following the usual Western approach, Barlaam began with the assumption that God was simple, unitary, and without division. Consistent with his opposition to the hyper-rationalism of Thomas Aquinas, Barlaam reasoned, in the Western way, that since God Himself was utterly transcendent and could not be known by rational means, He could only be known through His creation. On this basis, the hesychast's claims to 'know' God in an intimate way, particularly through participation in the Uncreated Light, were clearly deluded. He was willing to admit that the light they perceived might be an angel or some natural phenomenon – some part of the created order – but it could not be God. It could only be God if it was of the essence of God. But God's essence was invisible and unintelligible – incommunicable to human beings.

From the Athonite point of view, for which Saint Gregory became chief spokesman, Barlaam's account created too great a chasm between God and humanity. Had God Himself not come down to Earth in the great mystery of the Incarnation? Did not the tradition of the Fathers speak of a divinisation in which the purified and illuminated Christian became, in the words of St. Peter himself, *"sharers of the Divine nature?"* In the hesychast view, Barlaam's notion was closer to the Platonic conception of 'the One' or 'the Good,' a naked abstraction, as opposed to the Christian God Who chose to reveal Himself as Trinity. It also smacked too much of a Neoplatonic dualism in which 'spirit' and 'matter' were strictly opposed to one another. Patristic teaching emphasises the deification of the *whole person*, including *the body.*

From his monastic seclusion on Mount Athos, Gregory Palamas first wrote privately to Barlaam, trying to correct his misperceptions about hesychasm. Evidently failing to get an appropriate response, and meeting increased and continuing opposition, Gregory wrote this great theological and apologetic work, the *Triads in Defense of the Holy Hesychasts,* first on Mt. Athos and later in Thessaloniki. In 1340 - 1341, the council of the Mount Athos communities signed a text against Barlaamism which has since become known as the *'Hagiorite Tome.'* This document, written by Gregory, is now included in the great compendium of esoteric Christian texts, *The Philokalia.*

The controversy was by now a matter of public debate. The need arose for a formal resolution. A Council was convened under the auspices of the reigning Emperor, Andronicus III. It met at St. Sophia in Constantinople on June 10, 1341. Both Barlaam and Palamas were present and debated the questions openly. The Council decided the issues in favour of Gregory. His personal Christian qualities can be seen from the fact that, after the debate, Gregory and his friends greeted and congratulated Barlaam for a job well-done.

Barlaam returned to Italy shortly after this event. He converted to Roman Catholicism, and was appointed Bishop of Gerace. History last glimpses Barlaam toward the end of his life giving Greek lessons to the young Petrarch. He quickly leaves the historical stage of the 'hesychast controversy,' although his position was taken up by other contestants.

Just five days after the June 1341 Council, the Emperor Andronicus III, a supporter of Palamas, died. This precipitated a period of civil war, with two main parties vying for the throne of Byzantium. As happened frequently in Byzantine history, theology became entangled in politics, with Palamas becoming identified with the political faction of John VI Cantacuzenus. In this highly charged atmosphere, the controversy surrounding the hesychasts continued, despite the findings of the Council. A second Council met in Constantinople in August 1341, and Palamas again won the day, but political winds were, temporarily, blowing in contrary directions.

In this second phase of the conflict, Palamas' main opponent was Gregory Akindynus, a Bulgarian Slav. Akindynus, an acquaintance of

Palamas, had originally tried to mediate between Barlaam and the Athonite, but, being convinced by the former's arguments, emerged as a chief representative of the 'anti-Palamite' group. After 1346, Barlaam's ideas were championed by his former opponent Nicephoras Gregoras. Although a friend of Palamas' patron, John Cantecuzenus, Gregoras remained a bitter, and almost fanatical opponent of the hesychast monks until his death in 1360.

Associated with a political faction in civil war, Palamas was arrested and imprisoned on the orders of the Ecumenical Patriarch in 1343. Despite the findings of the two previous councils, he was excommunicated in 1344. As the tide turned and the political and military fortunes of John Cantacuzenus (crowned co-emperor in May 1346) began to rise, the eventual rehabilitation of Gregory Palamas and the vindication of the traditions for which he stood became inevitable. In February 1347 the anti-Palamite Patriarch of Constantinople, John Calecas, was deposed. His place on the Patriarchal throne was assumed by Gregory's old friend from his days in Thessaloniki, Isidore, a hesychast. Immediately, Saint Gregory was freed from prison and his Orthodoxy re-established. In May 1347, he was appointed Archbishop of Thessaloniki. Civil war still raging in that city, so that he was unable to take his seat as Archbishop until 1350.

The end of the controversy came in 1351 when a final Council convened on May 28 of that year in Constantinople, with Saint Gregory hastily travelling from Thessaloniki. Again, Palamas' views carried the day. On August 15, 1351 in a ceremony at St. Sophia in Constantinople, a formal *tomos* was read vindicating the hesychast position. The *tomos* was signed by both co-emperors, and presented to the Ecumenical Patriarch. For all intents, since that time, Saint Gregory Palamas' position has been the accepted theology of the Orthodox Church.

Saint Gregory served as Archbishop of Thessaloniki until he departed this life in 1359. His homilies during this period emphasize social justice, as the saint had a special concern for healing the wounds of this city after a period of war and division: *"Blessed are the peacemakers: for they shall be called the children of God."*

A final noteworthy episode in Palamas' life finds him taken prisoner by Turkish pirates, who held him for ransom. During his captivity he engaged the members of the Sultan's family in conversation regarding the tenets of Islam, and is reported to have expressed his hope for understanding between Christians and Muslims. This mirrors the saint's tolerance towards members of the Roman Church, with whom he enjoyed a friendly correspondence – an open-mindedness which far exceeded that of many of his Byzantine contemporaries – even those who were much closer to Rome theologically than was Saint Gregory.

Gregory Palamas died on November 27, 1359. He was officially glorified as a Saint by the Ecumenical Patriarch Philotheus, his disciple and friend, in 1368, a mere nine years after his death.

THE TRIADS

The real fact is that *The Triads in Defense of the Holy Hesychasts,* written 1337 - 9, is only secondarily a polemical or apologetic work. In the form of an argument against the Westernizing views of Barlaam the Calabrian and his supporters, Saint Gregory presents an exposition of the great teachings of the Fathers on stillness, inner prayer, the Uncreated Light, deifying Grace, and the distinction between God's Essence and His 'Energies.' As the title implies, the book was composed in three volumes, each of which contains three parts. This volume presents the first Triad for the first time in the English language in its complete form.

Beyond the very 'Byzantine' mode of expression, the text presents special difficulties to the modern reader. For instance, reading the modern literature on the subject, it can appear as though 'Hesychasm' were 'invented' in the 14th century. There is no doubt that this epoch represented one of the most important of the periodic revivals of the inner teaching of the Early Fathers, a teaching that is *not* an adjunct to Christianity, but *is at its very heart.* It must be made clear that Saint Gregory Palamas and his Athonite contemporaries did not envision themselves as theological innovators. St. Gregory, even in drawing his controversial distinction between essence and energies, was merely making *explicit* what was *implicit* in the teachings of earlier Fathers. Even the breathing techniques and psycho-somatic methods which are often closely associated with 14th Century 'Hesychasm' were probably of much earlier origin. St. John Climacus (6th century) and St. Hesychius the Priest (8th or 9th century) both recommend combining the Prayer of the Name of Jesus with the breath. It is unlikely that they were speaking in metaphors.

The central difficulty in researching the history of the teaching represented by St. Gregory Palamas is that of relying on documentary evidence for an unwritten tradition. Notably, the eminent historian Sir Steven Runciman, a supporter of Mount Athos in our own times, begins his account of *The Great Church in Captivity* with the recognition that *"The Orthodox Faith of Eastern Christendom ... has always preferred to cling to esoteric and unwritten tradition."* This is the nature of its orthodoxy, so although it is easy to view Gregory as a relatively isolated figure from an obscure world of the past, addressing problems of interest to scholars who study long-dead empires, the fact is that Gregory Palamas is one link – albeit a very important link – in the long line of succession of the Fathers which, according to the contemporary abbot of the Athonite Monastery of SimonoPetra, *"comes forth from the action of the Holy Spirit."*

This line of succession still exists today, and, as experience shows, these 14th century words come to life only when one begins to come under the influence of this succession – and this is particularly the case with most Westerners, who are the heirs more of Barlaam than of Palamas. Under this influence, we read *The Triads* not as a relic of theological controversies of the past, but as a living document that speaks of a timeless present which you and I can enter with God's help.

A document such as this necessitates a double translation. It must not only be rendered from Greek into English, but also translated from an artifact of a past culture to an experiential record of a timeless teaching ... something that it represents so eloquently to those *"who have ears to hear."*

THE FIRST TRIAD - PART 1

*First Discipline: Discerning the two different
kinds of knowledge*

INTERIOR OR NOETIC SCIENCE

In view of what has just been written, it is not surprising to find this First Part of the *First Triad* dealing primarily with the nature of spiritual knowledge; with how this differs substantially from other forms of knowledge familiar to us today, and how we can begin to approach it in our times. What this actually means, of course, is that - properly understood - what this first part contains is surprising. Paradoxically, the kind of knowledge described is a true mystery in the classical meaning of the term, a kind of truth that, although essentially Christian, is almost entirely unknown within the churches today.

It is fair to say that this ancient Christian concept of knowledge is embedded in the mind-set of early Christianity. It existed in a world which believed and observed that as our state of consciousness can change, with enormous benefits not only to the changed individual, but to the society in which he lives. Secondly, we can say that this change was intimately linked as both cause and result of a special kind of knowledge that comes from outside the sensory world, and whose presence is a characteristic of a state of consciousness which was subtly different from what is now generally known by that term. If it is put into practical use in life, this knowledge, first defined by Saint Paul, changes our awareness of the world, and to change the *way we know the world* is the same as changing the world as we experience it.

It is the existence of this kind of knowledge - its genuineness and its criteria, as rigorous as those of science although quite different

27

from the latter - which explains the power of religion during the first centuries of the church, as well as the many centuries in which it maintained its authority over the mediaeval mind. To understand this part of Palamas' great work is to understand with clarity a kind of thinking almost totally unknown by modern man and the modern church. In his First Part, the author of the Triads touches on several factors that are important in approaching this question with serious intent, including the existence of two different kinds of 'wisdom.' The Greek word is *sophia*, a word of great significance in the Greek church. The primary church in Byzantium was Aghia Sophia – Holy Wisdom - in Constantinople, and the Cathedral in the centre of Thessalonika, where Palamas was Archbishop when it was the second-city of Byzantium, has the same name. One of these two forms of wisdom, says Saint Gregory, attains what he describes as the aim of human life. The other 'misses the mark.'

The hesychast tradition to which Gregory belonged at one time used paradox in a very Zen-like way. Palamas himself in this First Part of his work, has produced a paradoxical text. It is of great intellectual precision. (In his youth he was trained as an Aristotelian philosopher). But paradoxically in the *Triads* he uses that intellectual precision to make people aware of the dangers in the normal uses of intellect. You can say that on the one hand we have intellect as a state of *identification*, as the part of the mind with which we are identified. Intellect when the mind is in this condition functions in a certain way. When we break identification, then intellect functions in a different way. It retains what it has learned, but whenever it remains free of identification it functions in integration with heart and motor centre, and in relation to nous as the command-centre. It is when it is in this condition that the results differ quite remarkably from those normal to Western individuals. The difference in our state of mind is what we mean by a different consciousness.

But this key fact of the early gospel teaching is virtually unknown today in the churches of the contemporary West, who now often think in a way formed not by this spiritual consciousness, but by a humanistic form of reasoning that is essentially non-Christian in its origins and style.

TRIADS IN DEFENCE OF THE HOLY HESYCHASTS

THE FIRST TRIAD - PART 1

THE TEXT

THE FIRST TRIAD - PART 1

FIRST QUESTION

I have heard it said by certain people that monks too must study worldly wisdom, and that unless they learn this, it is impossible for them to avoid ignorance[1] and false beliefs. Even if they have achieved the highest level of dispassion, they say, we cannot acquire perfection and sanctity without seeking education everywhere, but above all from Hellenic paedeia,[2] for that too is a gift from God,[3] just as much as was the gnosis granted to the prophets and apostles through revelation.

These people say that this kind of education gives the psyche a knowledge[4] of created things and enriches the faculty of noetic knowledge,[5] which is the highest of all the powers of the psyche.[6] Not only does it drive out all evils from the psyche - since every passion has its origin and foundation in ignorance - but it also leads men to the knowledge of God, for God can only be known through the mediation of His creatures.

I was not at all convinced when I heard these views, for my small experience of monastic life had shown me that the opposite was true. But I did not know how to answer them, because these people claimed with pride that: *"We not only concern ourselves with the mysteries of nature, we measure the celestial cycles, and study the opposed motions of the stars, their conjunctions, phases, and ascendants, and consider what they mean, (and we take great pride in all this). Since the inner principles of these phenomena are found in the divine and original creative Nous, and the images of these principles exist in our psyche, we try our hardest to understand them and to overcome our ignorance about them by methods such as*

31

distinction, syllogistic reasoning and analysis.[7] *We do this because, in this life and after it, we wish to be conformed to the likeness of the Creator."*

Unable to answer these arguments, I remained silent towards these people; but now I beg you, Father, to instruct me in what I should say to defend the truth, so that, (following the Apostle's injunction) I may *"be ready to give an account of the faith that is in us."* [8]

1.1

Brother, according to the teaching of the Apostle " ... it *is well for the heart to be established in grace."* [9] But how can anybody describe in words the good which is beyond words? For this, you must depend on God for a Grace which does not come to the nous of those who show off their wisdom, thinking that they know everything.

So if you do not have an answer for these people, even when you assume that they do not know the truth, you should not be distressed. Your own conviction has a firm foundation in experience,[10] so you will remain absolutely firm and unchanging, being constantly sustained on a foundation of truth, while those who rely on logical proof will change their minds. (Although this will no longer be the case with you.) For *"every word argues with some other word,"* [11] so that each word can become the object of dispute, and as a result it is impossible to discover the purpose of their words. Because of this, the Greeks, as well as those wise ones[12] who followed their teachings, have been clearly shown to be forever refuting one another's statements. They allow each other to be refuted simply by apparent superiority in verbal argument.

1.2

It is my opinion that you can give a sufficiently appropriate reply to those who, all their lives, who interest themselves in profane philosophy and seek knowledge in worldly education, and who are so enthusiastic in their praise for it. Simply tell them: *"My excellent friends, in this way you will gain no more knowledge than ignorance."* Those who seek human glory, and give everything to obtain it, are more

32

likely to gain dishonour than glory, since you can never please the whole world. These wise ones who seek it say themselves[13] that they will reap more ignorance than knowledge by it, since opinions differ and fight against each other, and each has more enemies than supporters.

It is to be feared that these people will not find the reasons for their beliefs in the Creative Nous.[14] The Apostle indeed asks us: *"Who has known the Nous of the Lord?"*[15] Without these reasons,[16] the worldly wisdom will not allow them to discover any images of them in the psyche. The knowledge which pretends to discover the image of God in worldly wisdom is therefore false knowledge. When it obtains [this wisdom], the psyche itself does not become in any way like truth itself. As this knowledge cannot lead it to the Truth, the boasting of those who flatter themselves that they possess truth by this means is futile. So let them listen to Paul when he calls the worldly wisdom carnal,[17] and speaks of it as *'the knowledge which puffs up,'*[18] and as a *'nous of flesh?'*[19] How could the wisdom of the flesh provide the [divine] image to the psyche? *"Consider,"* he says, *"that among those who have been called, not many are wise according to the flesh, nor are many of them mighty, nor are many of them wellborn."*[20] Neither noble birth nor physical strength can render the psyche powerful or noble. Nor can the wisdom of the flesh add any wisdom to our thinking.

In actual fact, the beginning of wisdom is to become wise enough to distinguish and prefer what is serviceable, heavenly, and spiritual - which comes from God, leads towards God, and makes those who acquire it Godlike - from what is base, earthly, and useless.

1.3

Yet, as these people recognise for themselves, we have within us images of the reasons[21] which are in the Creative Nous. So what is it which, since the beginning, has made these ineffective? Is it not because of sin, and also our ignorance or misunderstanding of the commandments, or our contempt for them? Why do we need to be taught to see these images when they are already inscribed within us? Is it not because the passionate part of the psyche, rising up in evil, has corrupted them, turning the visual capacity of the psyche upside-down and away from the archetypal beauty?

If we want to keep our divine image and our knowledge of the truth intact,[22] we must abstain from sin, we must know the law and commandments not merely in theory, but by practising them, and we must 'persevere in all the virtues,' and in this way turn back towards God through prayer and true contemplation. Without purity, one would not be any less mad, nor any the wiser, even by studying [worldly] philosophy from Adam to the end. Yet even if you do not know this natural philosophy, if you purify and strip away the bad habits and evil doctrines from your psyche, you will gain the wisdom of God, which has overcome the world. Then you will enter joyfully into eternity[23] with *"God, the only wise one."*[24]

The doctrines to which I refer have nothing to do with the size or movement of the heavens and the celestial bodies, nor the effects these bring about. They are not concerned with the earth and what is around it, nor the metals and precious stones in its interior, nor the phenomena that are produced in the air following retention of the breath.[25] It is the Hellenic heresy that concentrates all its enthusiasm and interest on those who research the science of such things. Indeed, all the Stoics define this science as the aim of contemplation.

1.4

And today, you tell us, certain people scoff at the aim recommended to Christians, making the pretext that the unspeakably good things we have been promised for the age to come[26] are too modest a goal! As they only know speculative science, they wish to introduce that into the church of those who practice the philosophy of Christ. They say that those who do not possess scientific knowledge are ignorant and imperfect beings; that everyone must give themselves entirely to Hellenic studies, and should disregard the teachings of the gospels. (In fact these last do not in any way help to separate from the ignorance of their sciences.) So, because he totally ignored those sciences, they separate themselves in their mocking from him who said: *"Become perfect.[27] If one is in Christ, one is perfect,[28] and we preach to the perfect."*[29]

34

As for me, when I spoke of the purity that brings salvation, I did not simply mean separating from worldly ignorance. I know, in fact, that there is a blameless ignorance, and there is knowledge which can be criticised. So it is not that kind of ignorance which must be stripped away, but their ignorance of God and the divine doctrines. This is the ignorance our theologians have forbidden. If you conform to the rules prescribed by our theologians, and make your whole way of life better, you will become filled with the wisdom of God, and in this way you will become truly an image and likeness of God. Then you will have attained perfection simply by obeying the gospel commandments. Saint Dionysius, who described the *Ecclesiastical Hierarchy*, clearly defined this conformity to the doctrine of this Hierarchy when he said: *"As we teach the divine scriptures, assimilation and union with God are accomplished only by that love and sanctity which puts into practice the most venerable commandments."* [30]

If these words are not true, if a person could rediscover and perceive the [divine] image, transforming his character for the better and ridding his soul of the shadows of ignorance simply through worldly education, then the wise ones of the Greeks would have been more closely conformed to God. They would have seen God better than did the fathers who came before the Law, and the Prophets who were under the Law. For most of these were called to this dignity while they lived a rustic way of life! Did not John, the highest peak of the prophets,[31] pass all his life from earliest infancy in the desert? Is he not the person whom all those who abandon the world wholeheartedly follow as their model? This is absolutely clear. Then where in the desert were the schools of that futile philosophy which those people call 'saving?' Where were the voluminous books, and where are those who fill the whole of their lives reading them, and persuading others to do the same? Do we find in those books the rules of the solitary and virginal life of the holy hermits, with a written description of the struggles they have undergone, so as to encourage the reader to imitate them?

35

I will leave aside the man who was *"the greatest among the children of women."* [32] From his great height he was not in the least concerned with this education which some people now say leads to God. He had not even read the sacred books. So I leave all that aside! But why then did *"He Who is before all ages,"* [33] Who appeared after him, and *"came into the world to testify to the truth,"* [34] to renew the image, [35] and to make it rise again to the Archetype, why did He not effect this return by worldly methods?

Why did He not say: *"if you would be perfect, obtain a worldly education. Be quick to assimilate the sciences and learn the science of created things?"* [36] Why did He say instead: *"Sell all that you possess, give to the poor,* [37] *take up the cross, and make every effort to follow me?"* [38] Why did He not teach the proportions, the angles, the phases and deceitful conjunctions of the planets in their wanderings? Then could something which is unable to resolve physical problems remove the shadows of ignorance from our psyche?

Why is it that the disciples that He called were fishermen, illiterates, countrymen, and not those wise ones? Was it not *"to confound the wise ones of the age,"* as Paul put it? [39] Would He confound those who, according to these people, led us to Him?

Why did He *"make their wisdom foolish?"* [40]

Why has He *"judged it good to save those that believe by the foolishness of preaching."* [41] Is it not because *"the world did not know God by its wisdom?"* [42] And what have they learned, these people of whom you were speaking?

For the Word of God came in the flesh. The light appeared around *"He Who was made for us wisdom coming from God."* [43]

For He was *"the light which gives light to every man who comes into the world."* [44]

For, according to the chief of the Apostles, *"the day has dawned, and the morning star has risen in our hearts"* [45] ... in the hearts of believers. But these people need a special wick [46]

36

which will light their way out of the philosophies and knowledge of the world. This is what will lead them to the knowledge of God. Yet instead, they advise other men to grow old in vain, sitting beside a smoking lamp.[47] They tell them to cease purifying themselves in stillness by the control of thoughts, and to abandon the unceasing prayer which lifts us up to God.

1.6

Has it not yet been realised by their nous that it was by desiring the Tree of Knowledge, then tasting it, that we were driven out of the place of delights?

Because we did not want to watch over our nous and cultivate it according to the commandment, we gave ourselves up to the evil advisor, who got in there by fraud, and seduced us with the beauty of the knowledge of good and evil. And today, for those who do not wish to work on themselves, nor to guard their hearts according to the teaching of the fathers, he promises exact knowledge of the celestial spheres, moving and symmetrical, and of their properties. This knowledge too is both good and evil; it is good in its nature, but the intention of those who use it modifies it in one direction or another. More importantly, I will say here that the practice and the graces of different languages, the power of rhetoric, historical knowledge, the discovery of the mysteries of nature, the different methods of practising logic, the different viewpoints of mathematical science, the varied forms and measures of immaterial science ... all these things are at different times both good and evil. This is not only because the way they appear is a result of the thoughts of those who use them, so that they easily take a form shaped by the point of view of those who possess them. It is also because studying them is a good thing, but only to the measure that through it they develop sharpness of vision in the eye of the psyche.[48]

So it is bad for one who dedicates himself to this study to continue it until old age. The better solution is to become briefly involved, then to move our efforts onto something that is a higher good and very much more certain. Contempt for letters also brings great compensation from God.[49] This is what the 'Second Theologian'[50] said, about Athanasius the Great; that the profit which he had gained from his secular studies was that he [learned to] define what he now judged it good to despise. In his own words, whether he rejected or possessed this knowledge, he himself preferred Christ, and he enjoyed everything else equally.

1.7

But the Evil One, who is always looking for ways of wickedly turning us aside from what is higher, casts spells[51] in our psyches, then interlaces them almost inescapably with the ties that are most dear to men of vanity. To some he suggests vistas of deep and diverse knowledge, while to others he suggests wealth, false fame or carnal pleasures. His purpose is that we spend our whole lives seeking these things, and never have enough strength left to set our hand firmly to the education which purifies the psyche.

"The beginning" of this education *"is the fear of God."*[52] This brings to birth unceasing prayer to God in compunction,[53] with obedience to the gospel commandments. Once reconciliation with God is re-established through prayer and fulfilment of the commandments, the fear becomes love. The sorrows of prayer, transformed into joy, lead to the appearance of the flower of illumination. Then, like a perfume from this flower, knowledge of the mysteries of God is given to those who can retain it. This is education in true knowledge. A man addicted to the love of vain philosophy, wrapped up in its figures and its theories, never sees even the beginning of this, which is *the Fear of God*.

How can this enter his psyche? Even if it could, how would it be able to live in a psyche that is surrounded, bewitched, and enclosed by varied and conflicting arguments, at least until it says goodbye to all these things and gives itself entirely to the School of God, at last giving itself wholly to His love by following the commandment.[54] This is why it is good that the Fear of God is the beginning of wisdom and divine contemplation. This fear will not live in the psyche alongside other feelings. It drives them all out. Then it polishes the psyche by prayer, making it like a tablet ready to be impressed by the grace of the Spirit.[55]

This is also why Basil the Great recalled the words of Pharaoh to Israel: *"Ye are idle, ye are idle: therefore ye say, Let us go and sacrifice to the LORD."* [56] Comment: *"This is a good way to take it easy. Let us use it to pass the time! Indeed, the worst form of leisure is that of the Athenians, who never passed their time without speaking and listening to new things.*[57] *This leisure activity, which some people imitate as they pass their lives today, is pleasing to the wicked spirits."* [58]

Nobody has said that Basil the Great's words about this were no more than fine flights of dramatic rhetoric. We recall what he said, while he was explaining the proverb of Solomon which advises us *"To know wisdom and instruction; to perceive the words of understanding."* [59]

"Now," said Basil, *"certain men who devote their time to geometry, discovered by the Egyptians, or astrology, venerated by the Chaldeans, or who are in general interested in numbers and shadows and meteorology, have scorned the study of the divine words. Many of them, because of their zeal against these things, have grown old searching in vain. So they should apply discernment to the studies they make, seeking out useful studies and rejecting what is unintelligent or harmful."* [60] Do you see? He calls these worldly studies vain, harmful, and unintelligent, referring to the knowledge of these worldly sciences and all that comes from it. And as you said, certain people claim that this knowledge is the aim of contemplation and believe that it leads to salvation.

Basil, writing to Eustathius of Sebaste, laments that he had passed the greater part of his life studying these sciences. He says, *"As for me, I have devoted a long time to vanity and wasted nearly all my youth on the useless trouble I gave myself assimilating the sciences of a wisdom made foolish by God.*[61] *But one day, as if emerging from a deep sleep, I realised the uselessness of the wisdom of the princes of this world who came to nothing:*[62] *I wept for a long time for my pitiful life, and prayed to be given instruction on what to do."* [63] And have you heard his names for the education and knowledge which certain people today vainly seek to promote? They are called *"vanity,"* *"useless suffering,"* *"wisdom gone mad,"* *"abolished wisdom,"* *"wisdom of this age and of the princes of this age,"* *"wisdom which eliminates the life and customs that are true to God."*

This is why this lover of true wisdom repented of giving himself to this [false wisdom] without finding any instruction that would take him to the true wisdom.

1.9

But today, in your own words, there are people who reach I do not know what degree of impudence! They say that to concentrate on *Hellenic* education throughout one's life is no obstacle to perfection. They do not hear the words of the Lord which say the opposite: *"Hypocrites! You know how to read the signs of the sky. How can you not recognise the time of the Kingdom?"* [64] For the time of the eternal reign is come; the God who gives it is present among us. How is it, if they genuinely seek the renewal of the nous, that they do not come back to Him in prayer to receive the ancient dignity of the free man? Instead, they turn to those who have not been able to free themselves. Yet the Brother of God clearly said: *"If any of you lacks wisdom, he should ask God, who gives to all, and it will be given to him."* [65]

Is it possible that the knowledge which comes from worldly wisdom drives out of the psyche all the bad things that originate from ignorance, when even knowledge from the gospel teaching cannot do so? *"For it is not the hearers of the law who shall be saved,"* says Paul, *"but those who fulfil it."* [66] He who knows the will of God and does not obey it *will be more strongly punished,*[67] said the Lord, than he who does not know it. Do you not see that knowledge alone achieves nothing? And why speak only of knowledge of what we should do, or of knowledge of the visible world or of the invisible? No: even a knowledge of God, Who created all this, will not achieve anything on its own.

"What will we gain from the divine doctrine if we do not live a life pleasing to God, that way of life which our Lord came to cultivate on earth." [68] It is John, the theologian with the golden mouth, who says this. For not only is there no benefit from this kind of knowledge, but it will cause the greatest harm to people. Those people

40

who have argued in this way, as you report to me, are also its victims, because *"it is not come with the power of words, lest it should destroy the mystery of the cross."* [69] And *"That which does not speak with the persuasive words of human wisdom,"* [70] and *"that which knows nothing save Jesus Christ, and him crucified."* [71]

What does he (Paul) write in Corinthians? *"Knowledge puffs up pride."* [72] Do you see? The summit of evil, the crime most natural to the devil, pride, was born of knowledge. But if this is so, how can it be possible that all the passions result from ignorance? Does knowledge purify the psyche? Paul says: *"Knowledge puffs up pride, but love builds up."*

Do you see? There exists a kind of knowledge that is without love. It does not purify the psyche in any way, but kills it, as it lacks the love which is the head, the body, and the very root of all virtue. But how could this knowledge, which is not properly constructive, (as is love), allow us to be made in the image of Him who is good?

Then how could this form of the knowledge that, as the Apostle said, *'puffs up pride,'* belong to the domain of faith, instead of that of nature! If even knowledge like this *'puffs up pride,'* how much more will that which we have been speaking of do the same? For it is natural. It arises from the *"old man."* [73]

In fact, worldly education serves natural knowledge. It can never become spiritual unless it is allied to faith and love of God, and it can never become spiritual unless it has been regenerated not only by love, but also by the grace which comes from love. Then, it becomes different from what it was, new and deiform, pure, peaceful, tolerant, persuasive, full of words which sustain those who listen to them, and full of good fruits. It is this form that is called *"the wisdom from on high,"* [74] or *"the wisdom of God,"* [75] as it is in some sense spiritual. Because it is subject to the wisdom of the Spirit, it knows and receives the gifts of the Spirit.

As for the other wisdom, it is 'daemonic' and 'of the psyche,' says the brother of God. [76] Therefore it does not receive the gifts of the Spirit, because it is written: *"The man of the psyche does not receive the gifts of the Spirit."* [77] It regards them as foolishness, as delusions or false doctrine. It seeks to completely suppress the

41

greater part of them, carries on an open struggle to return to the sensory and, wherever it can, to introduce false doctrine about them. It even skilfully approaches certain of these gifts to use them for its own ends, as sorcerers do with foods sweet to the taste.[78]

1.10

Thus the knowledge which comes from worldly education is not only different from but contradicts true and spiritual knowledge. Yet it seems that some people are not only misled themselves. They also seek to mislead those who listen to them. They speak as if there is only one kind of knowledge, and claim that this constitutes the aim of contemplation. And here is a fact which will reveal to you something of the terrible depth of evil into which the worldly philosophers have fallen. The Evil One and his philosophers, who derive their skill in doing evil from him, have stolen one of our most useful teachings. To serve as a dangerous decoy, they use identical terms to ours: *'be attentive to yourself,'*[79] and *'know yourself.'*[80]

But if you try to find out what their aim is with this precept, you will find an abyss of false doctrine. They teach the transmigration of the psyche, saying that you cannot know yourself and so be faithful to the teaching unless you know the body to which you were previously attached, the place where you dwelt, what you did there, and what you heard there. [They say] that you learn these things through obedience to the evil spirit, who deceptively whispers them to us in secret! This, then, is where they with their *'Know yourself'* lead those who cannot clearly perceive the deception and think they speak just as our Fathers spoke!

This is why Paul and Barnabas were not unaware of the thoughts of the Evil One and his initiates, but absolutely disapproved of the woman who said: *"These men are the servants of the most-high God."*[81] What words can one say more pious than these? But they knew about the one who tries to make himself appear like an angel of light.[82] They knew that his servants counterfeit *"ministers of righteousness,"*[83] and that they reject the true word because it is not suited to a lying mouth.

So even when we hear these Hellenists saying pious words, we do not think that they venerate God. We do not number them among our teachers, because we know they have stolen these words of ours. This is why one of them said about Plato: *"Who is Plato, if not Moses speaking in Greek?"*[84] So we know that if they have something beneficial, they have obtained it from us without fully understanding it. After making enquiries, we also understand that they give it a different meaning.

And if one of the Fathers says the same thing as one of these worldly men, the similarity is only in words. The meanings are quite different. In fact, according to Paul, the one has *"the nous of Christ,"* [85] while the others at best express human reasoning, and: *"As far as the heavens are from the earth, so far is my thought from yours,"* says the Lord.[86]

Moreover, even if these people sometimes had a thought in common with Moses, Solomon, and their imitators, how will this be useful? What man who is sound of nous and belongs to the Church could draw the conclusion that their teaching comes from God, or could even say that these heretics who appeared after Christ had received their doctrines from God, simply because they had not muddled all the truth after they received it from the Church?

"Every good and perfect gift is from on high, coming down from the Father of lights," said the disciple of the light.[87]

But even if the living gifts which the heretics receive are not mutilated, how will the worldly man, himself a heretic, offer them to others without mutilating them? A living being, even if mutilated, is at least alive, but a god who does not create out of nothing, who did not exist before our psyches, nor before the matter which has its balance and form within itself, how could this be God? In the words of the prophet: *"Those gods, who made neither the earth nor the heavens out of nothing, have disappeared."* [88] And those who say that they are gods [have disappeared] with them.

As for those people they call *'theologians'* or *'teachers,'* and think themselves able to borrow their theological terms, is it necessary even to mention them? Is it necessary that we keep away from *"the light*

43

which lights every man who comes into the world,"[89] and wait for the terrible shadows of ignorance to illumine us, on the pretext that, just as serpents are useful, this is something useful for us? For the flesh of serpents is only useful to us if they have been killed, cut up, and used with reason as a remedy against their own bites.[90] Those who kill them in this way turn a part of these snakes against themselves, just as if they killed a new Goliath with his own sword, one who had taken arms, who had set himself up to oppose us, *who had cursed the army of the living God.*[91]

Yet they were educated in divine things by fishermen and unlettered men.

1.12

We do not forbid anyone to initiate himself in worldly education if he wishes, at least if he has not adopted the monastic life. But we would not advise anyone to devote himself to this unendingly, and we absolutely forbid them to expect any accurate knowledge of divine things from it, since it is not possible to extract any teaching about God from such an education.

For *'God has made it foolish.'* Not that He created it that way. How could light produce darkness? But He made it into folly, so that it could not be confused with His wisdom.

Pay attention here! For if we say this, we also appear to say that the Law given by Moses was cut short and made foolish by the appearance of the Law of grace. But even if the Law is not cut short because it comes from God, the wisdom of the Hellenists has certainly been rendered foolish, because that does not come from God. Even though nothing exists which does not come from God, the 'wisdom' of the Hellenists is a false wisdom. Even if the nous which discovered it, being a nous, comes from God, this wisdom in itself, to the extent that it has been diverted from its end, which is the knowledge of God, should not be considered to be wisdom, but rather to be an abortion of wisdom, wisdom against reason, wisdom gone mad. This is why the Apostle [Paul] said that it has been 'made foolish,' not of itself, but because it seeks the things of this age and does not know the pre-eternal God, nor wish to know Him.

44

It is after asking: *"Where is the contentious man of this age?"* that he immediately adds: *"God has made foolish the wisdom of this world."* [92] This means that, in appearing on its own, it appears to have acted without true knowledge, so that it was not really wisdom despite the name we give it. For if it had been wisdom, how would it have become foolish, and that by an act of God and His Wisdom appearing on earth? For, according to the Great St. Dionysius, *"the higher good does not oppose the lower good."* [93]

As for me, I would also say that noetic things are not weakened by one another, and I would add that all beautiful things see their own beauty strengthened by the appearance of the higher Beauty. How could this not be so, now that that very Power, the Source of Beauty, has appeared? We will not say that the 'second lights,'[94] by which I mean those natures that are above this world, have been made useless by the First Light Who illuminates them. Nor will we say that our reason and our intelligence, very much lower than those lights, but lights nevertheless, have become darkness on the appearance of the divine light, once this appeared *"to light every man who comes into the world."*[95] For he who sets itself against this Light becomes darkness, be he angel or man, because he is separated from His will, and so finds himself abandoned by It.

1.13

It was by opposing the wisdom of God that this wisdom became folly. If it had been capable of discerning and announcing the wisdom of God in creatures, if it had made what was hidden appear, if it had been an organ of truth driving out ignorance, if it had participated in the Object of His message as well as its Cause, how would it have been made folly by the selfsame One who gave this wisdom to creation?

How, in fact, would this blow that it received not be anything other than the means by which the Wisdom of God appeared on the face of the universe? How would He who has established peace in the whole world, and for each creature in particular, not fight against it, when on the one hand He was the source of true wisdom, and on the other hand, by His arrival, He had struck at this wisdom of foolishness, as well as at those who had received it?

Yet it was necessary that this wisdom was there, not to be made foolish, but to be accomplished according to the ancient Law. Paul wrote about this: *"Do we thus abolish the Law? Never! On the contrary, we confirm the Law."*[96] The Lord invites us to look closely at this, for it contains eternal life.[97] He also said: *"If you had believed Moses, you would have faith in me:"* [98]

Do you see the extraordinary agreement of the Law with grace? For this reason, when the true light appeared, the Law became still better, because its hidden beauty was revealed. But this is not so with the wisdom of the Greeks. It was clothed in elegant words, pleasant and insinuating so that it hides its foolishness, but once its foolishness was revealed, it became worse than ever and justly earned the name of folly. In this case, it was not acting above reason, (this is the mystical[99] name given to the wisdom of God,[100]) but foolishly, as a result of a lack of knowledge of the truth, since it had abandoned the end appropriate to simple human wisdom.

Not only did it abandon this [truth], but it strayed in the opposite direction, and persisted in telling lies and presenting them as truth. Thus, it sought to slander truth as if the truth were lies, and set the creation against the Creator.[101]

Today, too, its action consists in turning the scriptures of the Spirit against the Spirit, against spiritual works, and against spiritual men.

1.14

The foolish philosophy of the worldly wise neither comprehends nor reveals the wisdom of God. How could it be otherwise, when *"the world did not know God by it?"* [102]

But if Paul said elsewhere that *"knowing God, they did not glorify Him as God,"* [103] he, the heir and disciple of Peace, who finds that the supernatural Peace in us is given by Christ alone, is not arguing with himself, but is simply saying that if they have come to conceive of God, they have done so in a fashion that is not appropriate to God. They have not worshipped Him as the Creator of all things, as the Almighty, as the one whose vision extends over all, or as the unique Being, without beginning and uncreated.

This is why these sages have been abandoned by God ever since the time when they lived, as Paul has again shown when he said that: *"God gave them over to their reprobate nous,*[104] *because they adored creatures instead of their Creator."*[105] Also for rolling themselves in the mire of base and shameful passions. Even worse - O passion, O artifice! - they decreed laws and composed writings which act in harmony with the daemons and pander to the passions. Do you see that the philosophy of these philosophers was foolish from its beginning and in its very nature? Its folly was not acquired from outside them.

Because it opposed the simplicity of the gospel preaching, and because it did not have the truth, what had first been rejected by heaven was made foolish again when it came to earth. This is why the man who gives that philosophy the attention of his nous, hoping to be led by it to obtain the knowledge of God or to receive purification for his psyche, experiences the same ills as it does, and becomes foolish. The clear proof that he finds himself in this situation, the first proof, is that he does not accept the traditions which have reached us from the Holy Fathers in faith, and in their simplicity. He does not know that they are better and wiser than those which come from human investigation and reasoning, nor that they are shown by works, instead of being proven by words. And yet all those who have received these traditions, and have then reaped their fruits by experience, really know in themselves that *"the foolishness of God is wiser than men."*[106] They all know this, and are able to testify to it.

1.15

But this is only the first proof that these philosophers are in fact fools. The second is even more important. The power of that reason-rendered-foolish and non-existent wars against those who accept these traditions in simplicity of heart, and so it mistakes the words of the Spirit, as in the example of men who neglect them and so have set the creation against the Creator.

It turns against the indescribeable activities of the Spirit, which acts better than reason in those who live according to the Spirit, and attacks the Spirit by attacking such men.

The third proof, which is even more evident, is that these wise ones without wisdom claim that - like the prophets - they are made wise by God. Plato, writing in praise of such men, states this clearly as a principle, showing in the greater part of his panegyric that they were transported by joy. *"And he who comes,"* he says, *"to compose poetic works without the inspiration of daemons, will be imperfect both in himself and his works. But the work of the man who is self-possessed is eclipsed by that of the madman."*[107] It was also Plato who, having begun to speak about the nature of the world through the mouth of Timaeus, vows to say nothing which is not dear to the gods.[108] But how can a philosophy which is dear to the daemons be beloved of God and come from God? As for Socrates, a daemon accompanied and initiated him! It appears to be true that it was a daemon who said to him that he was the wisest of all![109] Homer exhorted a goddess to use him as her medium when he sang of Achilles' homicidal anger. He allowed the daemon to take him over as an instrument, representing the goddess as the source of his own wisdom and eloquence.[110]

For Hesiod, it was not enough to be subject to the action of one daemon, since he is the author of the *Theogonie*. That is why he drew to himself exactly nine at the same time, sometimes Pierie, sometimes Helicon. And, in effect, *"he was filled with all kinds of wisdom"* which they had given him, and *"meanwhile, he puts the pigs out to pasture on the mountainside and eats the laurels of Helicon."* For another man, a different god *"made him play with his strength."* Yet another said about himself: *"I have been tamed by a muse who makes prophecies."* Another made a vow that the whole choir of the Muses would dance together in his psyche,[111] and also that the daughter of the seven stars of Pieros gave him his teaching on the seven zones, the seven planets, and their characteristics. He claimed that Urania, the daughter of Zeus, taught him the rest of astrology, and whatever else he knew concerning the things of earth was taught by other gods, regarded by these people as guardians of things here below.

48

Then do you wish to make us say that those who speak freely about themselves in this way possess the wisdom of God? Certainly not. What matters is that we are concerned for ourselves and the true Wisdom, which will not enter a psyche that is full of craftiness and friendly to daemons. Indeed, if it has entered previously, it flies away whenever the psyche turns towards evil.

"The Holy Spirit of Instruction is repelled by thoughts that are without understanding,"[112] said Solomon, who possessed the wisdom of God and wrote a book on the subject. Is there anybody who lacks understanding more than people who boast that they are initiated into the mysteries of the daemons and who attribute the origin of their own wisdom to them? What we say now we would not say about philosophy in general, but only about the philosophy of such people. If, in fact, according to Paul, we cannot at the same time drink the cup of the Lord and the cup of the daemons,[113] how could someone possess the wisdom of God and still be inspired by daemons? That is not possible. Absolutely not! And if Paul actually said somewhere that *"... in the wisdom of God, the world did not know God,"*[114] then be careful! It is not the wisdom of these unwise sages which he has named *"the wisdom of God,"* but that which the Creator breathed into creatures.

Anybody who has recognised this wisdom as a messenger of God has recognised the God that it announces. Such a person possesses the true knowledge of created things, and so he possesses the wisdom of God. He becomes expert in the wisdom of God. *"It must be,"* says the great Dionysius, *"that true philosophers ascend by means of the knowledge of created things towards the origin of beings."*[115]

If a true philosopher ascends to the First Cause, he who does not ascend is no true philosopher. He does not possess wisdom, but only a sort of lying imitation of true wisdom, and this is not wisdom, but the negation of all wisdom. And how could we name the negation of wisdom the *'wisdom of God?'* Besides, the daemonic nous is a good thing when seen simply as nous,[116] but becomes bad whenever it is misused. While it is better than us at knowing the measurements of the world, the orbits, conjunctions, and definitions of moving bodies, it is a nousless nous, full of darkness, since it does not use its knowledge in a way that pleases God.

In the same way, this Hellenic wisdom thinks it can base itself on the Wisdom of God found in created things, by which God transforms the corruption of a being through the birth of another being - to show that God is not the Lord of all things, nor the Creator of the universe! But it does not see that everything always has an origin! It therefore turns aside from the veneration of the true God. According to the same Dionysius the Great, it *"irreligiously opposes itself to divine things,"* [117] and so becomes a foolish and insane wisdom. How could this be the wisdom of God?

This is why Paul shows us that wisdom has two forms. He says: *"In the wisdom of God, the world has not known God through wisdom."*[118] Do you not see that he spoke on the one hand of wisdom which is of God, and on the other, simply of wisdom, which causes ignorance of God? This last is what the Greeks discovered. It is different from that of God, and the evidence is in the two little further on? *"We teach the wisdom of God."*[119]

Do the Greeks agree with him, or does Paul agree with them? Not at all! This is why he excludes the possibility of any such agreement and says: *"We preach a wisdom among the perfect, a wisdom which is not of this age, nor of the princes of this age who are coming to nothing,"* [120] This is a wisdom *"which none of the princes of this world have known."* [121] This last wisdom is found in us in Christ Jesus, *"who has been made by God for our wisdom."* [122]

As to the other wisdom, it was not in these people but in the creatures they were studying. They investigated it all their lives and reached a certain conception of God, for nature and creation give great opportunities for this. The daemons, in a thoroughly daemonic way, do not hinder this. Indeed, how could they have been taken for gods if the thought of God had never entered human reason?

By examining the nature of the objects of sense perception, these people have arrived at a certain concept of God, but not at an understanding truly worthy of Him and appropriate to His blessed nature. For their *"insane heart was darkened"*[123] by the activities of the wicked daemons who communicated obscene teachings to them. Indeed, if a correct concept of God had appeared in the thought of these philosophers, how would they have believed it when the daemons presented their polytheistic teaching? How could anybody take daemons for gods? Yet, entangled in this foolish wisdom and uninspired education, they slandered both God and nature. They gave rulership to nature, at the same time depriving God of His sovereignty, (at least as far as they are concerned). They attributed the Divine Name to daemons. So far were they from finding the knowledge of created things - the object of their desire and zeal - that they claim that inanimate things have a psyche, or that they participate in a psyche higher than our own.[124] Then, by saying that they can contain a human psyche, they claim that unreasoning things possess reason. They then claim that the daemons are greater than we and - O impiety! - that they are our creators. They not only classified matter and all of what they call the World Soul, with everything else uncreated or causeless, as coeternal with God, but also anything noetic which is not clothed in the density of a body, even our psyches.

Then are we going to say that those who believe this philosophy have the wisdom of God, or even normal human wisdom? I hope that none of us would be mad enough to say this, for, as the Lord said, *"A good tree does not produce bad fruit."*[125] As far as I am concerned, I do not think that this 'wisdom' is even worthy to be called 'human.' It is so inconsistent that it describes the same things at the same time as both animate and inanimate. It says both that they have and that they lack reason. And it says that things whose nature is without sensibility, and which have no sensory organs, could contain our psyches![126]

Paul sometimes speaks of this wisdom as *'human wisdom,'* as when he says, *"My preaching does not rest on the persuasive words of human wisdom,"*[127] And again, *"We do not speak in words which teach human wisdom."*[128] But he also thinks it right to call those who have

51

acquired this wisdom *"wise men according to the flesh,"* [129] or *"wise men become fools,"* [130] *"the disputants of this age,"* [131] and their wisdom is qualified by him in similar terms: It is *"wisdom become folly,"* the *"wisdom which has been done away,"* *"empty deceit,"* [132] the *"wisdom of this age,"* and it belongs to the *"princes of this age, who are coming to an end."* [133]

1.19

For myself, I listen to the father who says, *"Woe to the body which does not ingest nourishment from outside itself, and woe to the psyche which does not receive grace from above itself!"* For the body will perish once it has been transformed into an inanimate being, and the psyche, once it turns away from what is proper to it, will be caught-up with daemonic life and daemonic thoughts.

But if someone says that philosophy, in the sense that it is natural, is a gift from God, then they speak the truth, without contradicting us. But this does not cancel out the accusation of those who abuse philosophy and pervert it to an unnatural end. For they make their condemnation greater when they use God's gift in a way that does not please Him. Even the nous of daemons was created by God, and so it naturally has understanding, but we do not hold that its activity comes from God, even if the possibility of action comes from Him. We could honestly call that kind of reasoning unreasonable. [134] The nous of the worldly sages is also a divine gift, to the measure to which it naturally possesses a wisdom capable of reasoning. But when it puts forward doctrines like these, it has been perverted by the devil's wiles, which have transformed it into foolish wisdom that is wicked and unaware. [135]

So if someone tells us that the desire and knowledge of the daemons themselves is not entirely bad - since they desire to exist, to live, and to think - here is the best reply for me to give: There is no need to argue against us because we say, (with the brother of the Lord,) that Hellenic wisdom is 'daemonic' [136] because it arouses quarrels and contains almost every kind of false teaching, and because it is alienated from its appropriate end, that is, from the knowledge of God. Because we recognise that, even in this state, it may participate in the good in a remote and indistinct manner, we should remember that nothing evil is evil because it exists, but only when it has been turned aside from the activity appropriate to it, and so from the end belonging to that activity.

1.20

So what should be the work and goal of those who seek the wisdom of God in creatures? Is it not to acquire truth and to glorify the Creator? This is evident to everyone. But the knowledge of those worldly sages falls short of both these aims.

Then is there anything which may be of use in this philosophy? Certainly there is great therapeutic value in substances obtained from the flesh of serpents,[137] so that doctors consider that there is no better and more effective antidote than that, and, just as when people prepare poisons with the intention to deceive and use the sweetest foods to hide their deadly nature, there is also some benefit to be had even from words of the worldly wise - in a way it is similar to a mixture of honey and hemlock. But we must take care that those who seek to separate the honey from the mixture do not mistakenly drink the deadly remnant.

If you examine the problem, you will see that most of the harmful heresies originate in this way. This is what happens with the 'iconognosts.' They pretend that man receives the image of God as knowledge, and that it is this knowledge that conforms the psyche to God. But it was said to Cain that *"If you make your offering correctly, without dividing correctly..."*[138] Very few men are able to divide well. People only 'divide well' when the sensitivities of their psyches are trained to discern right from wrong.

But why do we need to run these dangers in vain, when it is possible to contemplate the wisdom of God in His creatures with profit, and not just without peril?

When hope in God has liberated life from every care, this naturally impels our psyche to understand God's creatures: Then it will be filled with admiration, will deepen its understanding, and continually glorify the Creator. By this miracle it will be led forward to what is above. According to St. Isaac, *"It finds treasures which cannot be expressed in words."*[139] Then it is that it uses prayer as a key, penetrating with this into mysteries which *"eye has not seen, ear has not heard, and which have not entered into the heart of man."* [140]

St. Paul teaches that these mysteries are revealed by the Spirit only to those who are worthy.

1.21

Do you see the shortest way, which leads us to these supernatural and heavenly treasures most profitably and without danger?

If you begin with worldly wisdom, on the other hand, it is first necessary to kill the serpent, after overcoming the pride that comes to you from this philosophy. How difficult! No wonder it is said that: *"The arrogance of philosophy has nothing in common with humility."* After you have overcome it, you must separate and throw away the head and tail,[141] for these things are the extremities, and they are evil in the highest degree. By the head, I mean manifestly wrong opinions concerning things noetic, divine, and primordial. By the tail, I mean assumptions about created things. As to what lies between, that is, discourses on nature, you must separate out harmful ideas by using the abilities in critical analysis and observation belonging to your psyche, just as pharmacists purify the flesh of serpents with fire and water. But to do all this, and make good use of what has been properly set aside, much effort and much judgement will be required!

Nonetheless, if you put to good use that part of the secular wisdom which has been clearly separated from the rest, no harm can result, for now by its nature it will have become an instrument for good. Even so, it cannot in the strict sense be called a gift of God and a spiritual thing, for it is derived from the order of nature. It is not sent from on high.

This is why Paul, who is wise concerning all things divine, calls it 'carnal;'[142] for, says he, *"Consider that among us who have been chosen, there are not many of us who are wise according to the flesh."* [143] Who could make better use of this wisdom than those Paul calls *"externally wise?"* [144] But having this wisdom in their nous, he calls them *"wise according to the flesh."* The term is appropriate!

In lawful marriage, the pleasure whose aim is procreation cannot truly be called a gift of God, because it is physical and given us by nature, not by grace, (even though that nature has been created by God). In the same way, the knowledge derived from exterior education, even if it is well used, is a gift of nature and not of grace. It is given by God to everyone without exception. It is a part of our nature, and we can develop it by exercise. This last point - that nobody acquires it without effort and exercise - is evident proof that it is a natural gift, and not spiritual. It is our sacred wisdom which is properly called a gift of God. That is not a gift of nature. Even simple fishermen who receive [this wisdom] from on high become, as Gregory the Theologian says, sons of thunder,[145] whose word encompasses the very bounds of the universe.

By this grace, even publicans are made merchants of souls; and even the burning zeal of persecutors who receive it is transformed: Saul became Paul,[146] and turned away from the earth to attain *"the third heaven"* and *"hear indescribable things."* [147] By this we too can become conformed to the image of God, so that we will continue in this form after death.

As to natural wisdom, it is said that Adam possessed it in abundance, more than any of his descendants, although he was the first of all those who failed to safeguard our conformity to the divine image. On the other hand, the worldly philosophy existed to serve this theosophy before the advent of Him who came to recall the psyche to its primordial beauty. But why were we not renewed by it before the advent of Christ? Why did we need, not a teacher of philosophy - of an art which passes away with this age, so that it is said to be *"of this age"* [148] - but One *"who takes away the sin of the world,"* [149] and who gives a true and eternal wisdom - even though this appears to be 'foolishness'[150] to the short-lived and corrupt wise men of this world? It is the lack of this which makes those who do not attend to it in their nous truly foolish? But can you not see clearly that it is not studying the worldly sciences which brings salvation. This does not purify the cognitive faculty of the psyche, nor make it into a likeness of the divine Archetype.

I will draw an appropriate conclusion from what I have previously said on the subject. If a man who turns toward the prescriptions of the law to seek purification gets no help from Christ - even though the Law has clearly been given by God - then neither will learning the worldly sciences help.

Then will it not be true too that Christ is of no help to someone who turns to the rejected philosophy of the worldly men to gain purification for his psyche? It is Paul, the spokesman of Christ, who tells us this and gives us his testimony.

Now, brother, this is what you must say to those who give too much importance to worldly wisdom. In the passages we have transcribed below we shall show them in another way how futile and trivial this appeared to our holy Fathers, particularly to those who have experienced it.

From the Bishop of Nyssa, taken from his *'Contemplation on the formation of the body.'*

This is the law of the spiritual sheep: never to heed the voice which speaks outside the Church, and, as the Lord said, 'never listen to the voice of a stranger.'[151]

From the same, from his *'Letter to Eupatros'*

Your zeal for reading about worldly matters proves to me that you do not care about the divine sciences.[152]

From Basil the Great, taken from his *'Commentary on the seventh Psalm'*

We have discovered two meanings to the word 'truth.' One refers to understanding the ways leading to the blessed life, the other is the proper understanding of many of the phenomena of the world. The first truth contributes to our salvation. It is present in the hearts of the perfect, who transmit it unchanged to those around them. But if we do not know the truth about the earth and the sea, the stars, their movement, and their speed, this will not prevent anybody from reaching the promised beatitude.[153]

From Dionysius the great, an extract from the first book of his *'Heavenly Hierarchy'*

In the teaching of the divine scriptures, assimilation and union to God is only accomplished by love and holiness that puts into practice the most venerable commandments.[154]

From Chrysostom, from his *'Commentary on the Gospel of Saint Matthew'*

What in the past the exteriorly wise could not imagine even in their dreams, fishermen and unlettered men have told us with full certainty. Having turned their backs on the earth, they speak of all that can be found in the heavens. They bring us a new life and a new existence; freedom, servitude, a new world, and everything different, but not in the manner of Plato, of Zeno, or of those who composed the laws. The very personality of these last has shown us that an evil spirit and a primitive daemon which turns against our nature instructed their souls. As for the fishermen, they teach us about God in knowledge that no philosopher could ever convey to our nous. So the knowledge of these philosophers is in the past and has disappeared for good reason, for these are the doctrines of daemons. They have disappeared because they are held in contempt, having less value than cobwebs. They are the objects of derision, impudent, full of shadows and futility. But the doctrines we [give] you are not of this kind.[155]

From Saint Gregory the Theologian

The first wisdom is a life praiseworthy and purified by God; a life on the way to being purified by the Most Pure and the Most Luminous One, by Him who asks of us only one sacrifice, purification. The first wisdom is to scorn the 'wisdom of words' that takes the form of verbal refinements and deceitful and misleading contradictions. This first is the wisdom which I praise; it is this which I seek: the wisdom by which fishermen, after having overcome the 'wisdom reduced to nothing,' have captured the entire universe in the net of the gospels, with their perfect and concise words.[156]

From Saint Cyril, extract from his *'Commentary on the Ninth Psalm'*

Those who have practiced the worldly, daemonic and animal wisdom boast about themselves and plunge those with limited intelligence into the fire. They make them the sons of Gehenna. They speak in favour of lying. With their glib tongues they make their ruse attractive and succeed in fooling many people who are taken

58

with the advice of these charlatans and fall into their nets. All their counsels are snares and entanglements to trap those without education.[157]

From the Bishop of Nyssa, extract from his *'Commentary on Ecclesiastes'*

See the syllogistic demonstration of Ecclesiastes! It says that much knowledge accompanies much wisdom, and that an increase of sorrow follows an increase of knowledge.[158] So the acquisition of the many superfluous sciences of those in the world, as well as the highest human wisdom and knowledge acquired by pain and long hours, do not bring anything necessary or useful, nor anything that earns eternal life for those who have dedicated so much zeal to these things. Instead, it earns them even greater pain.

So we must say goodbye to all that, be vigilant in chanting, in prayers, and in supplications addressed to our own Creator, our God and our Master, attach ourselves firmly, and commit our time to Him.

In order that our useless occupations may not condemn us to even a brief delay in the school of vanities, we must lift up our hearts and nous to the incomprehensible height of the divine majesty with the help of this kind of exercise. By participation and communion in which we abandon ourselves to the inexpressible glory - to the measure that it may be contemplated and imagined - we must fix our attention on the beauty of the sun of glory, and allow it to illumine us men inwardly and outwardly. Then we will be filled with inexpressible divine joy.[159]

THE FIRST TRIAD - PART 2

Second Discipline: Entry into the heart

"I sleep, but my heart waketh: it is the voice of my beloved that knocketh, saying, Open to me, my sister, my love, my dove, my undefiled: for my head is filled with dew, and my locks with the drops of the night." [1]

A 'PSYCHOLOGICAL METHOD'

In Part Two of this book, Palamas provides certain basic concepts of what has more recently been described as a 'Psychological Method,' specifically the hesychastic interior discipline taught and used by many of the early fathers of the Eastern churches and still taught by their successors today. Until now, this tradition has been only incompletely adapted into the West. Most recently, it formed part of the 'Fourth Way' teaching, despite the fact that this lacks any mention of the essential divine element. But the Palamas text shows how the efforts of the individual relate to the grace of God: how man's contribution opens us to the saving divine grace, and how, even before that, man is wakened to self-amendment by God, an amendment that bears fruit through the loving action of the Spirit in prayer and communion.

In reconciling these disparate streams, Saint Gregory not only potentially heals the breach which in the West has weakened the link between laity and monastics, introducing a stream of theology with a still dwindling awareness of ascesis. He also shows us, in potential, how this great breach in modern Christianity could be healed. From him we can learn how the disciplines once normal to the more devout Christians could be re-established, making uneccessary the flight from the church to one or another of the Eastern traditions of those who seek such a discipline, an inner discipline, more like Yoga, Zen, or Sufism, which once existed in the church, and in which the existence of the practical exercises which once existed in every major faith have remained generally recognised and continue to be intact and effective.

Concentrating on the inner sense of the hesychastic ascesis, the second - and shortest - of the three parts of Palamas' First Triad gives what seems to be the clearest and most complete definition of the spiritual methods of the early fathers. This section provides initial instruction in the practical techniques used in spiritual life to establish and deepen our watchfulness. In it, there is knowledge that is not readily available to modern Christians, even among those whose lives are dedicated to spirituality. Indeed, some of it may never have been fully understood in the West. The original understanding of it was certainly lost to us many centuries ago, for the instruction given in this part of the book provides the key to a complete system of inner development. That system has been around much longer than the seven hundred years that have passed since this text was written, and is a method that is rooted firmly in the teaching of the gospels.

THE EARLY CHURCH

In concentrating on the nature and practice of watchfulness, this second part of Gregory Palamas' first Triad concentrates its attention on the second of the three main stages of the Christian spiritual path, each of which might be regarded as separate disciplines. It lays the technically exact foundation of one of the great methods of the ancient Christian spiritual discipline defined by Saint Paul, and shows certain of the reasons for a system of practices that long before Palamas' time had included traditional Prayer of the Heart. This is still taught today in more or less the same form, mainly by monastics of the Orthodox church, and was once described to me by the Abbot of one of their communities as 'the principal export of Mount Athos.' These exercises, which include physical posture as well as 'noetic prayer' or prayer of the heart, can be looked at in one sense as the equivalent in the inner dimension of everyday work in the outside world.

They form what at first sight is a direct equivalent of those of the Indian Yogas which lead to God Realisation, but in fact this method is very different from any of the Indian methods now widely taught in the West. In most forms of Yoga as taught in the West, the primary effort is one of individual discipline - for instance the Raja Yoga of Patanjali begins by sorting out external life, then progresses to dealing with the body, then the psyche, and finally the nous, a process in which the effort of the pupil appears to be the major element. The ancient Christian disciplines, on the other hand, often emphasise that the effort begins from the heart as a kind of dialogue in which the Spirit calls to the heart of the individual, and that heart has to waken and respond.

The process in each case is fundamentally similar, but the approach is different. It appears that all Christian methods are centred on the heart.

This part of the First Triad describes how, by directing the nous back into the heart, the God-seeker must progressively take up the reins of the psyche, and it is this process which appears so much like the disciplines used in Yoga. The process even passes through similar phases, leading eventually to the awakening of a form of what is known in the Western churches as *infused contemplation,* in which the action of the nous and the connection with the Spirit feeds the heart, informs it, and takes command of it in order to complete the individual's transformation so that we can say with David: *"The shadows are no longer dark, thanks to you, and night for me will be as clear as day now that you have taken possession of my reins."* [2]

TRIADS IN DEFENCE OF THE HOLY HESYCHASTS

THE FIRST TRIAD - PART 2

THE TEXT

TRIAD 1 - PART 2 - THE TEXT

SECOND QUESTION

You have done well, Father, to have brought up these quotations from the saints concerning my question. In listening to you to resolve my uncertainty, I have enjoyed this evidence of the truth. But one thought keeps insinuating itself into my mind. Since *"every word argues with every other,"* as you yourself have said, would it not also be possible to argue against your own words? Yet I know that the testimony of works is incontestable, and I have heard that the saints say just what you say, so I will think no more about this. If someone is not convinced by the saints, how would he be capable of faith? How would he not reject the God of the saints? For it was He who said to the Apostles – and they said it to the saints who followed them - that: *"he who rejects you rejects me,"* [3] that is, he rejects truth itself. And how should those who reject the truth reach agreement with those who seek the truth?

I ask you now, Father, to hear my explanation of each of the other arguments which I have understood are put forward by these men who pass their lives occupied with Hellenic education. I also ask you to tell me whatever you judge best about them, and to add the opinion of the saints on the subject.

These people say, in effect, that we are wrong when we wish to enclose our nous within our body. Instead, they say, at any price we must cast it out of our body. They strongly criticise some of our people, and write against them, under the pretext that our people encourage beginners to look into themselves and to introduce their nous into themselves by means of breathing practices. They say that if the nous is not separate from the psyche, how can we bring into ourselves something that is not separate from us but is part of our psy-

friends of ours speak of introducing divine grace into themselves through the nostrils. But I know that this is an active attempt to slander us, for I have heard nothing about this in our milieu.[4] I must conclude that their conduct is equally misleading in other domains, as those who make false accusations also distort reality.

But you, Father, please teach me: why do we try so hard to bring our nous into ourselves? Why do we not think that it is wrong to shut it away in our body?

2.1 – PALAMAS' SECOND ANSWER

Brother, have you not heard that the Apostle says, *"Our bodies are the temple of the Holy Spirit which is in us,"*[5] and again, *"We are the house of God?"*[6] For God Himself says, *"I will live in them and I will walk in them and I shall be their God."*[7] Then why should anybody who possesses nous be indignant at the thought that our nous dwells in something whose nature is to become the dwelling place of God? How then would God have caused the nous to inhabit the body in the first place? Was He also wrong? The truth is, brother, that these words apply more properly to heretics. They apply to those heretics who claim that the body is an evil thing made by the Wicked One.[8]

As for us, we believe it is a bad thing for the nous to be caught up in carnal thoughts. But it is not in itself wrong for the nous to be in the body, since the body is not evil.[9] This is why all those who have been attached to God all their life cry out to God, with David: *"My soul thirsteth for thee, my flesh longeth for thee,"*[10] and *"my heart and my flesh rejoice in the living God."*[11] And with Isaiah: *"My stomach resonates like a zither, and my entrails like a bronze shield which has been rebuilt as new,"*[12] and also, *"by the fear that we have of You, Lord, we have conceived in our entrails the Spirit of your salvation."*[13]

Because we have confidence in this Spirit, we will not fall. It is those who speak the language of earth who will fall, those who say falsely that the words and life of heaven are just like those on earth. For if the Apostle, too, calls the body *'death,'* (in fact, he said: *"Who will deliver me from this body of death?"*[14]) it is because material and corporeal thought really takes its form from the body. There, to

70

contrast it with spiritual and divine thinking, he rightly calls it *'body;'* and not simply body, but *'body of death.'*

A little earlier he had showed more clearly that he does not accuse the flesh itself, but that sinful desire which overcame it later because of the fall. *"I am sold to sin"*[15] he says. But he who is sold is not a slave by nature. And again: *"I know that what is good does not dwell in me, that is, not in my flesh."*[16] He does not say, do you see, that it is the flesh which is evil, but what dwells in it. What is evil is not the fact that the nous lives in our body, but an evil power, *"the law which is in our members, which struggles against the law of the nous."*[17]

2.2

This is how we turn against this *'law of sin.'*[18] We expel it from the body, and instead we introduce supervision[19] by the nous, and by this authority we bring each power of the psyche, and every member of the body[20] which will respond to it, under the rule of the nous.

For the senses, we determine the object and the limits of their actions. This work of the law is called *'self-control.'*[21]

For the passionate part of the psyche, we achieve the best state of being, which bears the name of *'love.'*[22]

We also improve the rational part, by eliminating all that prevents the thoughts from turning towards God. That part of the law we name *'watchfulness.'*[23]

Someone who has purified his body by self-control, someone who by divine love has made his wilfulness and his desires a means of virtue, someone who presents to God a nous purified by prayer, acquires and sees in himself the grace promised to those whose hearts are pure. He can then say with Paul: *"For God, who commanded the light to shine out of darkness, hath shined in our hearts, to give the light of the knowledge of the glory of God in the person of Jesus Christ."*[24]

But, he says, *"we carry this treasure in earthen vessels."*[25] In consequence, in order to know the glory of the Holy Spirit, we carry the light of the Father, in the person of Jesus Christ, in earthen vessels, that is to say, in our bodies. So will we then fail to achieve nobility of nous if we keep our own nous in the interior of our body? Even without divine grace, what man who has a human nous - I won't even say what spiritually awake[26] man - could say this?

2.3

The psyche is one, yet it has many powers. It makes use of the body, which lives naturally in conformity with it as an organ. But what organs does this power of the psyche which we call the 'nous' use when it is active?

Nobody has ever supposed that the nous was in the fingernails, in the eyelids, in the nostrils or the lips. Everyone agrees it is found inside us, but some people hesitate to be specific. Can the breast or the belly be its primary organ? Some people, in effect, place the nous in the brain as if in a kind of acropolis.[27] Others consider that its vehicle is the very centre of the heart, that part of the heart which is free of the animal breath.[28]

For ourselves, we also know by exact experience that because it is incorporeal, our reason is not inside us, in the way it would be inside a jar. Nor is it outside us, because it is part of us. But it is in the heart as if in its organ. We do not learn this from a man, but from the very Creator of man, who taught that *"it is not what enters, but what comes out of the mouth, that defiles a man,"*[29] and He also said: *"For it is from the heart that evil thoughts come."*[30]

The great Macarius did not say anything different: *"The heart,"* he said, *"rules the whole organism, and when grace possesses the heart, it rules over all the thoughts and all the members; for the nous is there, as well as all the thoughts of the psyche."* [31]

So our heart is the seat of reason,[32] and the primary reasoning organ of the flesh. Consequently, we seek to examine and rectify our reason by rigorous watchfulness. But with what would we watch it, if we had not gathered our nous there after it had been scattered abroad by sensations. With what would we watch it, if we did not bring it back to the interior of this same heart that is the seat of our thoughts?

This is why Macarius, so justly called 'the blessed,' immediately goes on to say: *"We must look to see if grace has engraved the laws of the Spirit there."* [33] Where? In the organ of control, the throne of grace, where we find the nous as well as all the thoughts of the psyche, that is to say, in the heart.

Do you see now how very necessary it is for those who have decided to attend to themselves in stillness[34] to gather their nous and enclose it in the body, and especially in this body that is the deepest part of the body, which we call the 'heart?'

2.4

If, as the Psalmist says, *"the king's daughter is all-glorious within,"* [35] why do we search for her outside?

And if the Apostle says, *"God gave His Spirit to cry in our hearts, Abba, Father,"*[36] how is it that we too do not pray in the Spirit within our hearts?

And if, as the Lord of the prophets and apostles teaches, *"the Kingdom of Heaven is within us,"*[37] if we apply all our energy to make our nous turn outside us, will we not find ourselves outside the Kingdom of Heaven?

For *"the true heart,"* says Solomon, *"looks for perception."* [38] In another place, he calls that perception *"noetic and divine."* All the Fathers seek this perception,[39] for they repeatedly say that: *"The intelligent nous continually seeks to acquire noetic perception, so let us not cease to seek that sense, within us and outside us."*[40]

Do you see that if we desire to combat sin and acquire virtue, to find the reward of the struggle for virtue, or rather the noetic perception, pledge of that reward,[41] we must bring the nous back into the body, and into itself? The opposite, to look for noetic visions by making the nous 'go out,' not only from thoughts about the flesh, but out of the body itself - that is the greatest of the Hellenic errors, the root and source of all corrupt doctrine. This doctrine engenders folly and is the result of mad foolhardiness, an invention of daemons. This is why those who speak by daemonic inspiration find themselves beside themselves, not knowing what they are saying.[42]

As for us, we not only recollect our nous into our body and then within our heart, but within itself.

73

Then there are those who say that the nous is not separate from the psyche but is interior to it. For this reason, they question how we can possibly recall it into ourselves. It seems that these people are ignorant of the fact that the essence of the nous is one thing, its activity another. Or rather, they are well aware of this, but prefer to side with the deceitful and play on the ambiguity. *"Such men, sharpened to contradiction by dialectic, do not accept the simplicity of the spiritual teaching."* As the great Basil says: *"They distort the force of truth with opposing arguments of false knowledge,*[43] *aided by the persuasive arguments of sophistry."* [44] These people must conclude that they are able to judge spiritual things[45] and even teach them, even though they themselves are not spiritual!

It should not have escaped them that in fact the nous is not like the eye, which sees the different visible objects but cannot see itself.

The nous operates in one way in its function of exterior observation: (This is what the great Dionysius calls the movement of the nous *"along a straight line."*)[46] It has another way in which it comes back to itself, then acts from itself when it becomes aware of itself. This movement the same Father calls *"circular."*[47] This is the most excellent and appropriate activity by which the nous comes to transcend itself and become united to God. *"For the nous,"* says St. Basil, *"when it is not dispersed abroad,"* (Notice how he says "dispersed?" What is dispersed, then, needs to be recollected. That is why it is pursued.) *"returns to itself, and then, through itself, mounts towards God"*[48] as if by an infallible road. Dionysius, that infallible observer of things noetic, says that this movement of the nous is not subject to any error.[49]

The Father of Lies always wishes people to abandon this ascent, so that their delusions will lead them to fulfil his plan for them. Until now, (as far as we know), he had found no collaborator who had made the effort to lead others to this goal by facile talk. But now, as you tell me, it seems he has accomplices who have even composed treatises towards this end, and who seek to persuade men, (even those who have embraced the higher life of Hesychasm,) that it would be better for them to keep the nous outside the body during prayer.[50] These people do not even respect the clear and authoritative words of John, who writes in his *Ladder of Divine Ascent,* that: "The *Hesychast is someone who seeks to enclose the bodiless in his body.* "[51]

Yet our spiritual fathers have passed the same teaching down to us, and rightly so, for if the Hesychast does not enclose the nous in his body, how can he have within himself He who clothed Himself in a body; He who, in His natural form, penetrates all organised matter? For the exactly defined exterior form of matter is not compatible with the essence of the nous until the moment when that matter becomes alive, having achieved a form of life that is shaped by union.[52]

2.7

You see, brother, how John teaches that it is enough to examine the matter in a human (let alone a spiritual) way, to see that when you decide truly to belong to yourself - to be a monk[53] who is inwardly worthy of the name, and is in accord with the interior man - then it is absolutely necessary to recall or keep the nous within the body.

On the other hand, it is not inappropriate to teach beginners, especially, to observe themselves and to send back their nous into themselves by following the inspiration of the breath. A man of understanding will not forbid someone who has not as yet achieved self-awareness to use definite methods to bring [the attention of] his nous back within himself.

Those who are only beginning this struggle find that their nous, when recollected, continually becomes dispersed again, being brought back only with difficulty. It is therefore necessary for such people to bring it back into themselves continually; but in their inexperience they fail to grasp that nothing in the world is in fact more difficult to observe and more mobile and shifting than the nous. Thus it is not out of place to teach people, especially beginners, that they should observe themselves and introduce their own nous into themselves by controlling their breathing.[54] This is why certain people recommend controlling the inward and outward movement of the breath, and holding it briefly.

In this way they will be able to hold their nous steady by watching their breath - at least until, through the grace of God, they have made progress, have restrained their nous from becoming distracted by what is around it, keeping it clear and unconfused, and so have truly become capable of leading it to *'single-pointed concentration. '*[55]

At the same time, we can say that control of the breath is a spontaneous result of the attentive state of the nous. The in and out movement of the breath becomes peaceful at any time of intense reflection, especially in those who practice stillness in body and in thought.

In effect, people like this practise a spiritual Sabbath. As far as they can they avoid all personal action. They strip the powers of the psyche of every changing, mobile, and diversified knowledge, of all sense perceptions, and, in general, of all bodily activity that is under their control. As far as possible, they restrain even actions which are not entirely under their control, like breathing.

2.8

In the case of those who have made progress in hesychasm, all this occurs without painful effort, and without the need to think about it, for the complete entry of the psyche within itself necessarily and spontaneously produces it. But with beginners, none of these things happens without a struggle. As patience is a fruit of love (*"for love bears all,"*[56] and we have been taught to practice patience with all our strength to come to love), so it happens here. But why say any more about this? Those who have experience can only laugh when contradicted by the inexperienced. Their teacher was not words, but work, and the experience which comes from their own efforts. It is this last which bears useful fruit, and it is this which renders sterile the points-of-view of the tricksters and accusers.

One of the great doctors teaches, *"Since the transgression,*[57] *the inner man automatically adapts to exterior forms."*[58] Thus, the man who seeks to turn his nous back into itself need not propel it in a straight line, but into the infallible circular motion.[59] How will he not gain great profit in this if, instead of letting his eye roam hither and thither, he should fix it on his breast or navel as on a pin-point of concentration? [60] Taking the outward form of a circle in this way, he will not only collect himself, but will conform himself to the interior movement that he seeks for his nous. In addition, by taking this attitude in his body, he will send the force of the nous - which otherwise escapes into the exterior through the sight - back into the interior of the heart.

If the power of the noetic animal[61] is situated at the centre of the belly,[62] where the law of sin exercises its rule and gives it pasture, why should we not exert *'the law of the nous, which struggles with"* [63] this power, at just that place, armed with prayer? Then the evil spirit, who has been driven away by the *'bath of regeneration,'* [64] will not return to install himself there with seven other spirits more evil than himself, making *"the latter state worse than the first."*[65]

2.9

"Attend to yourself," says Moses,[66] meaning, to yourself as a whole, not just a part while ignoring the rest. How? With the nous, evidently, for we cannot be attentive to ourselves as a whole with any other power. But if you post a guard over your psyche and body, it will easily deliver you from the evil passions of both body and psyche. So attend to yourself, take a grip on yourself, be aware of yourself, or rather mount guard over yourself, take command, master yourself! For this is how you will make the disobedient flesh submit to the Spirit, so that *"there will never again be a lying word in your heart."* [67]

"If the spirit of him who rules" - that is, that which has authority over the evil spirits and harmful passions - *"rises within you,"* as Scripture says, *"do not leave your place,"*[68] in other words, never leave any part of your psyche or any member of your body without keeping watch over it. In this way, you will become unapproachable to the spirits that attack you from below, and you will be able to present yourself confidently to *"Him who searches the reins and the heart;"*[69] and that without His examining you, because you will have examined yourself. You will then have the blessed experience of David, and will say to God: *"The shadows are no longer dark, thanks to you, and night for me will be as clear as day, for you have taken possession of my reins."* [71]

David says, in effect, *"Not only have you made all the* desires *of my psyche your own, but if there is a spark of desire in my body it has returned to its source, it is attached to you by that origin, raised and united to you."*

Those who abandon themselves to sensual and corrupting pleasures centre all the desires of their psyche on the flesh, so that they become entirely 'flesh.' It is then, (as the Scripture says,) that the Spirit of God cannot dwell in them. But in the case of those who have elevated their nous to God and exalted their psyche through divine longing, their flesh too is transformed and elevated.[72] Then it participates in the divine communion and becomes the dwelling and possession of God. It is no longer the seat of enmity towards God, and no longer possesses any desires opposed to those of the Spirit.

2.10

Between the flesh and the nous, what is the most direct link for that spirit[73] which arises in us from below? Is it not the flesh which, as the Apostle said, does not enclose anything good until the law of life has come to live in it? For the strongest reason, then, we must never relax our attention towards it. So how do we make sure that it becomes our own, so that we do not lose it?

Unless we train ourselves in our exterior posture so as to keep watch over ourselves, how can we prevent the Evil One from rising up in us, we who do not yet know how to reject spiritual evil by spiritual means?

And why have I spoken about novices, when the most perfect adopt this posture during prayer and so attract to themselves the benevolence of God? Certain of them lived after Christ, but others preceded His coming. Elias himself, the most perfect of those who had seen God, leaned his head on his knees and so with a great struggle gathered his nous into himself, bringing to an end a dryness of many years.[74]

But these people, brother, who you say speak in this way, appear to suffer from the disease of the Pharisees. They do not wish to observe and purify the interior of the vessel,[75] that is to say, their hearts. They despise the tradition of the Fathers and seek to take precedence over everybody like new teachers of the law. Yet they themselves disdain the form of prayer that the Lord had justified in the case of the publican, and they advise others not to practice this form of prayer. But in the Gospel, the Lord actually said: *"He didn't even dare to raise his eyes to heaven."*[76] Those who seek to turn their vision back into themselves in their prayer correctly imitate the publican. Some people call them 'omphalopsychics,'[77] intentionally maligning them as if they were adversaries. Yet who among them ever said that the psyche was in the navel?

2.11

These people clearly use slander as a way of presenting themselves. More than this, they openly insult those worthy of praise, all the time pretending that they are simply correcting their mistakes. It is not the cause of the hesychast life or of the truth which drives them to write, but their vanity. It is not the desire to lead people towards watchfulness, but to lead them away from it.[78] They endeavour by all these means to discredit the work of watchfulness, as well as those who devote themselves to it, finding an excuse for this in the practices which are linked to it. These people would be ready to treat as if they were coeliopsychics[79] anyone who said: *"The law of God is in the middle of my stomach,"*[80] as well as the person who once exclaimed: *"My stomach resonates like a harp, and my entrails like a bronze shield which has been rebuilt as new."*[81] They slander without distinction anybody who employs corporeal symbols to represent, define, or study things that are noetic, divine, or spiritual.

But the saints do not suffer at all by this. Instead, they receive praises and crowns without number in heaven, while these people wait outside the sacred veil, and can't even ponder the shadows of the truth.[82] And it is strongly to be feared that they will pay for this by eternal judgement, not only because they separated themselves from the saints, but because they attacked them with words.

You know the Life of Symeon the New Theologian. Almost from beginning to end it was a miracle. God glorified him by supernatural miracles. You also know his writings: if you describe these as 'words of life' you are not lying in any way. You know of Saint Nicephorus, who spent long years in the desert, in hesychia. Afterwards he lived in the most deserted parts of the Holy Mountain, and while he was there he allowed himself no respite. It was he who transmitted the practice of watchfulness to us, having collected it from all the writings of the Fathers.[83] These two saints taught[84] clearly - to those who have chosen this way - the practices which certain people, as you reported to us, are now fighting against.

But why speak only of the saints of the past? These men who testified a little time before us, and who are recognised as having possessed the power of the Holy Spirit, have passed these things on to us out of their own mouths. That theologian, for example, the 'True Theologian,' who most certainly contemplated the true mysteries of God, was celebrated in our time. I speak of Theoleptus, who was truly 'inspired by God,'[85] the Bishop of Philadelphia, who illumined the whole world like a candelabrum. And that Athanasius who for many years ornamented the patriarchal throne and whose tomb was honoured by God. And Nilus, originally from Italy, imitator of Nilus the Great, Seliotis, and Ilias, who were in no way inferior to him. Then there were Gabriel and Athanasius, who had the gift of prophecy.

It is about all these that I would speak, and about many others who were before them, with them, and after them. They exhorted and encouraged those who wish to guard this tradition. At the same time, these new teachers of hesychasm wish to admonish us, not from experience, but as part of their boasting, since they do not know even a trace of hesychia. These people seek to reject the same tradition, to distort it, to make it appear despicable, all without giving any benefit to those who hear them.

80

Speaking for ourselves, we have personally conversed with certain *saints, and they were our teachers.[86] So what does this matter? Should we count as nothing those who have received the teaching of experience and of grace? Yet you would have us bow before those who are themselves led to teach only by their pride and their search for verbal debate. That will not be. Never!

And you, keep yourself away from these people and address yourself wisely with David when he says: *"Bless the LORD, O my soul: and all that is within me, bless his holy name."*[87]

Let yourself be convinced by the Fathers. Study everything that they advise you about the way to make your nous turn back into your inner self.

THE FIRST TRIAD - PART 3

Third Disicpline: Illumination and the Charismatic Light

AN ANALYSIS OF INTERIOR EXPERIENCES

The third part of Gregory Palamas' first *Triad* refers precisely to the third of the three stages of the Hesychastic path. It describes the way we can directly experience the action of the divine within us. To the Hesychast, and to many other people who follow the teachings of the early fathers of the church, it is this experience which is known as *the knowledge of God*. It is the product of the progressive awakening of the new, emotional consciousness.

Thus this third part of Gregory Palamas' *Triads* is so directly related to Christian inner experience that it provides what might be called an experimental solution; a clearly defined statement of the testable elements of that doctrine. It is experimental in the sense that any Christian who develops the necessary spiritual expertise can also investigate these states of consciousness and being, and can then compare their own experiences against Palamas' description.

In this context, it is important to note that this text was not peripheral to the teachings of the church. In a time of political troubles that included the progressive conquest of the Eastern part of the Roman Empire by the Turks, and in which social confusions spilled over into theology, the doctrines of Palamas were approved in the Imperial Councils of the church, and can be seen as in agreement with the doctrines of the Council which – in 1351 - gave final form to those doctrines. In referring to 'testable elements' of the doctrine we also mean that the rendering of the Greek words into consistent terms in English - with a very few necessary deviations - reveals that this section of Palamas' book provides a coherent and internally consistent terminology for the elements of the Christian mystical psychology and mystical and charismatic experience. This means that all the terms used are clearly explainable in terms of each other, just as are all the terms of the physical sciences clearly related to each other. However, while the physical sciences create their theoretical models by combining experimental observations and individually developed meta-concepts drawn from a variety of sources or simply invented, the classical Christian theoretical models taught by the early fathers of the church drew from a single coherent 'doctrine.' They did so in such a way that the total representation is testable by the individual under certain conditions. These conditions are in fact referred to in the first two parts of this first *Triad*, and are two in number:

By putting the ideas into practice we learn the meaning of the doctrine. By observing the results of that practice, we confirm its validity.

These are the 'scientific criteria' of the interior science of the early church. Because, apart from the visible light of the Transfiguration experience discussed later in this section of the book, they are only accessible to individuals and not to collective demonstration, they tend to be undervalued. Those with experience easily grasp what is meant when they are described, but those without experience have difficulty. Intellectual studies play little part in this process, except where they lead those who are habitually aware only of externals to turn their attention inward.

TRIADS IN DEFENCE OF THE HOLY HESYCHASTS

THE FIRST TRIAD - PART 3

THE TEXT

THIRD QUESTION

I understand better now, Father, that the accusers of the Hesychasts not only lack the knowledge that comes from spiritual practice, but even ignore what they learn from their experience of life, the only thing that is certain and irrefutable. They even refuse absolutely to listen to the words of the Fathers. *"Puffed up with futile pride,"* as the Apostle says, *"in their nous of flesh they busy themselves with things they have not seen."*[1] They are so far from the right way that, while they openly criticise the saints, they cannot agree between themselves about anything. That is why they choose to speak about illumination, although they actually consider that any illumination which is accessible to the senses is an illusion, and at the same time, say themselves that all divine illumination is accessible to the senses. For instance, they claimed that all illuminations that occurred among the Jews and their prophets, under the Old Law and before the coming of Christ, were only symbolic. But they also say that the illumination on Tabor at the time of the Saviour's transfiguration, and the one when the Holy Spirit descended, and all similar phenomena, were clearly perceptible to the senses. Again, according to them, *knowledge*[2] is the only illumination that transcends the senses, so they claim that this is superior to the light. Thus they believe that knowledge forms the end of all contemplation.

Next I shall briefly describe to you what they claim to have heard said by people around them. I beg you to help me, and to accept that I have never heard anything like this among the Hesychasts, and cannot persuade myself that these people could have heard such things around one of our people. But they say that they pretended to enter the school of the Hesychasts without accepting their teaching. Then they wrote down what these teachers said in order to attract and persuade them. They wrote that these masters suggested that they should entirely abandon sacred Scripture as something evil and attach themselves to prayer alone. They claim that not only did these teachers say that prayer drives out evil spirits which have been mingled with the very being of people, but that when this happens they become inflamed in a perceptible manner, leap about, and are filled with feelings of pleasure, all without their psyches being in any way changed. Then they see sensible lights, and have come to think that the sign of divine things is a white colour, and that evil things are a fiery yellow.

While they wrote that those teachers spoke in this way, they themselves said that all this is daemonic. And if anyone contradicts anything they say, they say that this is a sign of passion, which in turn is a mark of delusion.[3] They throw numerous reproaches in the faces of their adversaries. In their writings they imitate the many convolutions and perfidies of the serpent, turning back upon themselves in many ways. They use many ruses, and interpret their own words in different and contradictory manners. They do not possess the firmness and simplicity of truth, but easily fall into contradiction and, ashamed at the accusation of their own conscience, seek, like Adam, to hide themselves in complication, conundrums, and ambiguities about different meanings of words. I therefore pray, father, that you will clarify our opinion of their views.

3.1 - THIRD ANSWER

Not only are vices planted alongside virtues, but even their impious words appear to be so close to pious words that a small addition or subtraction is enough to easily transform one into the other. In this way, the meanings of the words can be completely changed. This is why nearly all wrong opinions wear the mask of truth. This will deceive anyone who does not notice the small additions or omissions. This is the dangerous means used by the evil daemon, so skilled in the art of deception. Telling a lie close to the truth, he invented a double ruse: The small distance is not noticed by most people, who easily take a lie for the truth or the truth for a lie when it is close to it. In both cases this completely separates us from the truth.

Initiated in this art, the partisans of Arius in the town of Nike[4] opposed the written definition of the faith of Nicea, shamefully treating that which *"correctly divided the word of Thy truth."* Arius himself used this ruse. He very nearly concelebrated with those who had repudiated him before the church and received communion. But the great Alexander, having discovered the trick but unable to refute it clearly, turned to God in prayer and, in that way, justly delivered that disgraceful man to an infamous death. He was truly carried away by his own lunacy.

3.2

This, brother, is the ruse which is most often used by those who speak as you describe. Beginners in Hesychasm find themselves advised to avoid too much reading. They are to give themselves to the prayer of a single word[5] until unceasing prayer becomes the normal state of their thinking,[6] even if they have moved on bodily to another occupation. The students find the same counsel given by Saint Diadochos, Philemon the Great, Nilus, so rich in things divine, John, the author of the *Ladder*, as well as many fathers now living. This is not because reading is either useless or wrong. But these people added this word 'wrong,' and by doing this, they made the good advice of the fathers seem to be something that is actually harmful.

Among other things, we know that all the saints have shown in their words and their actions that prayer drives out evil spirits and passions. All the wise men think this and teach it, but none of them ever said that these evil spirits had become merged with our essence. By making this arbitrary addition, those who spoke to you made the aim of our efforts seem wrong.

The great Basil himself said that the heart should leap as if palpitating with enthusiasm for love of the Good. Athanasius the Great said that this was a sign of grace. The author of the *Ladder* clearly teaches that when, with an unpolluted nous, we have a meeting with God, we come out of prayer like a body of flame. Without this, without the presence of light in prayer, without the sweetness it brings to the psyche, the prayer, he thinks, is corporeal or 'Judaic.' And a number of others, notably Saint Isaac, have showed clearly that a reflection of joy will appear on the faces of those who pray, and not only as a result of inner prayer, but also when they are chanting in full awareness.

The principle behind[7] of all this is the need to improve the reasoning psyche,[8] yet these critics of the saints you speak about have rejected what is praiseworthy, and have made it the object of blame. Having mutilated the sure testimonies of sacred and divine illumination, they have hidden behind small details which favour their accusations and - alas - attempt to make the inexperienced think that the divine is in reality daemonic.

But above all, they are convinced of the fact that *"those who are hidden in the eternal shadows"* [9] produce the light, although in a misleading way. Yet they do not admit that God is beyond all illumination and all light, nor do they say that He fills all reasoning natures with a noetic light that is capable of apprehending light that is of noetic origin like itself.

3.3

For me, I think that knowledge, which you tell me these people say is the only noetic illumination, is called light only to the measure to which it is communicated by the divine light. According to the words of the great Paul: *"For God, who commanded the light to shine out of darkness, hath shined in our hearts, to give the light of the knowledge of the glory of God..."* [10] In his turn, the great Dionysius too said: *"The presence of the noetic light unifies those it illumines, and reintegrates them in the one true knowledge."* Do you see? The light of knowledge is communicated by the presence of the light of grace, and liberates us from the ignorance which fragments us. This father called this light 'noetic,' [11] while the great Macarius, clearly concerned with those who assimilate the light of grace in the form of knowledge, names it 'perceptible to the nous!' [12]

"By its effects," he says, *"you will see if the noetic light which has shone in your psyche, comes from God or Satan."*

Elsewhere, after having called the glory which had appeared on the face of Moses 'immortality,' (although it illumined a mortal face), and showing how it appears in the psyche as soon as we truly love God, Macarius said: *"As the visible eyes see the visible sun, so it is with the eyes of their psyche that these men see the noetic light which reveals itself and will shine from their bodies at the moment of Resurrection, to make them resplendent with eternal light."* [13]

As for the light of knowledge,[14] we may never say that it is 'noetic.' To the contrary, that light sometimes acts like a 'noetic' light. At those times, the nous 'sees' it as an intelligible 'light' through its 'noetic' sense. When it enters reasoning psyches, it liberates them from the ignorance which bound them to their state, bringing them back to unified knowledge from multiple opinions. This is why the Cantor of the Divine Names, when he begins to sing the luminous names of the Good, teaches us to say that: *"The Good is named the noetic light because it fills every nous above the heavens with noetic light, and because it drives out all ignorance and all illusion from every psyche it enters."* [15]

So the knowledge which comes after ignorance has been driven out is one thing, while the noetic light which makes this knowledge appear is another. This is why the noetic light is manifestly present in the 'nous above the heavens,' that is to say, in what has transcended itself.

How can we describe the light which is above the heavens and above the nous as 'gnosis,' except in metaphor? To put it another way, only the reasoning psyche could purify itself of the ignorance due to its state, which that great doctor described as 'ignorance' and 'illusion.'

3.4

When it is victorious over the passions, the human nous, like the angelic, can transcend itself and become like an angel. It will then

93

find the light, and will become worthy of a supernatural vision of God. It does not see the essence of God, but it sees God by a revelation that is true to Him as well as appropriate to itself. This is not through verbal negation. One really sees it, but this seeing is superior to negation, for God is not only beyond knowledge, He is even beyond unknowing.

His revelation is truly a mystery in itself, the more divine and extraordinary since, the divine manifestations, although they are symbolic, remain unknowable in their transcendence. In fact, they appear according to a law which is neither that of divine nature nor of human nature - being, as it were, for us and yet beyond us - so that there is no name which can properly describe them. And this God showed very well when, in reply to Manoe's question, *"What is your name?"* He replied, *"It is marvellous,"* for this vision is no less marvellous, not only because it is incomprehensible, but because it cannot be named.

Moreover, although this vision is above negation, the words which describe it are inferior to the negative way. The latter progresses by using examples and analogies, which is why we most often add the word 'like' to the words we use to express it. This is in order to make a closer likeness, since the vision itself is inexpressible and beggars all description.

3.5

The saints[16] contemplate this divine light within themselves, seeing it through the divinising communion of the Spirit, with the mysterious accompaniment of inspired illuminations. It is then that they see the garment of their deification, as their nous is glorified and filled by the grace of the Word in an extraordinary outpouring of beauty. This was how, on the mountain, the divinity of the Word glorified His body with the divine light which shone from it. For He Himself has given *"the glory which the Father gave Him"* to those who are obedient to Him, as the Gospel says:[17] *"He willed that they should be with Him and contemplate His glory."*

94

But how could this happen physically when He Himself was no longer physically present after His ascension into heaven? Instead, it must necessarily happen in a noetic way as the nous goes beyond the heavens.

Then it becomes the companion of Him Who ascended into heaven for us.

Then it unites itself to God and contemplates supernatural and inexpressible visions filled with all the immaterial knowledge of a sublime light.

Then it no longer contemplates the sacred symbols accessible to the senses, nor any longer knows the variety of the Holy Scriptures.

Then it is made beautiful by the creative and original beauty, and illumined by the light of God.

In the same way, according to the one who revealed and interpreted their *Hierarchy*, the sublime orders of the cosmic spirits beyond the heavens have arranged themselves hierarchically not only according to their relation to the original experience and knowledge, but also to the light first seen in the sublime triadic initiation. Not only did they gain participation in and contemplation of the glory of the Trinity, but also of the light of Jesus which was revealed to the disciples on Tabor.[18]

Judged worthy of this vision, they receive a true initiation, for that light is also a deifying light. They truly come closer to Him and receive their first communion from his deifying radiance. This is why the truly blessed Macarius called this light the *"food of beings beyond the heavens."* And here is what another theologian says: *"All the nous-bearing array of beings beyond the cosmos, immaterially celebrating this light, give us clear proof of the love which the Word bears towards us."* [19]

And the great Paul, at the moment of meeting the invisible and heavenly visions in Christ, was 'ravished' and found himself beyond the heavens, yet his nous did not actually need to move to a different place. He did not need to change his position to pass beyond the heavens. For this 'ravishment' denotes an entirely different mystery, known only to those who have felt it. And it is not necessary to say today what we have heard on the subject from the fathers who have had this experience, for we do not wish to expose them to slander. But what has now been said will be enough to show very clearly, to those who are not convinced, that there is a noetic illumination visible to those who have purified their hearts. This is completely different from knowledge, but it can bring knowledge.

3.6

As you yourself have told us, these people have said that the illuminations described in the Old Testament have a symbolic character. They have showed clearly that there is a holy illumination of which this is a symbol.

Saint Nilus[20] teaches that most of these are symbols of this illumination, saying: *"when the nous, after it has put off the old man, has clothed itself in what is born of grace, then, during prayer, it will see its own state like a sapphire or the colour of the sky; Scripture calls this 'the Place of God,'*[21] *which the ancients saw at the foot of Mount Sinai."*[22] In the same way we hear Saint Isaac say to us: *"The nous, when grace acts on it, sees its own purity in prayer, like the celestial colour which the community of Israel called the Place of God when it appeared to them on the mountain."*

Do you not see how these illuminations are symbols of what can happen now in pure hearts? And John - golden in tongue and thought - explained the words of the Apostle: For *God, who commanded the light to shine out in darkness, hath shined in our hearts;"*[23] according to him, the Apostle shows that *"the glory of Moses shone in us even more strongly, for it has shone in our hearts as it did on the face of Moses."*

And he says further down: *"At the beginning of creation, He spoke and there was light. Today He did not speak, but he Himself has become our light."*

So, if the light at the beginning of creation or that which shone on the face of Moses was a limited form of knowledge, the illumination which occurs in our hearts would also be knowledge, but greater because it has been developed. But since the light was not knowledge, but a radiance appearing on his face, the radiance it produces in us is also not knowledge, but a radiance of the psyche appearing to the purified nous.

So one light, visible to the eyes of the senses, is itself sensible, while the other is noetic and acts within us, where only noetic eyes have access to it.

3.7

Yet that light was not simply a light of the senses, although it appeared on the face of the prophet. According to Saint Macarius, in fact, the saints of the present day receive in their psyches the same glory that appeared on the face of Moses. This same father also called this light the *"glory of Christ,"* and regarded it as being above the senses, although it appeared accessible to sense. With a small addition, he puts forward this word of the Apostle: *"All of us who, with face uncovered, contemplate the glory of the Lord, that is to say, his noetic light, as if in a mirror, are transformed in the same image from glory to glory, that is to say by the increase in the light which is in us and which, under the influence of the divine light, becomes ever more distinct."* [24]

What does Saint Diadochos say? *"You should not doubt that, when the nous begins to feel the action of the divine light frequently, it becomes so completely translucent, it sees the abundance of its own light vividly. When the strength of the psyche makes it mistress of the passions, it becomes all light."* [25]

And what does the divine Maximos say? *"A human nous would never have the power to ascend and so participate in the divine illuminations if God himself had not exalted and illumined it with divine radiance."* [26]

What does Nilus say, with the divine Basil? *"The Cappadocian Basil, that illustrious pillar of truth, affirms that all human knowledge is simply study and practice, while the knowledge coming from the grace of God is justice and mercy."* [27]

"The first of these can be acquired by the passionate," adds Saint Basil, *"while the second is only received by those who have conquered the passions; who see the radiance of their nous illumine them even outside the time of prayer."* Do you understand clearly, brother, that when the nous is freed from passions, it sees itself during prayer as a light, and shines with divine light?

So lend a docile ear and listen again to the truly blessed Macarius. He, whom the most divine Nilus called a *"chosen vessel,"*[28] says, in the *Chapters* paraphrased by Metaphrastes, that: *"'The perfect illumination of the Spirit is not only a revelation in noetic thought, but a certain and continuous illumination of hypostatic light in the psyches.'* This is well confirmed by passages such as this: *'He who commanded the light to shine in the heart of darkness has shone in our hearts.'*[29] And it says: *'Illumine my eyes, lest I sleep the sleep of death;'*[30] and again: *'Send out Your light and Your truth and let them guide me to Your holy mountain.'*[31] Also there is: *'The light of your countenance is come upon us as a sign.'"*[32] And there are many similar passages."[33]

Here, he said 'hypostatic' to stop the mouths of those who consider that illumination is simply knowledge,[34] and as a result sow confusion in the thoughts of many people - and first of all in their own. They do this by wrongly interpreting all that is said about that light in just the way in which we have already described in the case of knowledge. But I know that knowledge is also called 'light,' because it is derived from the light, since it is produced by that last. I said this earlier on.

3.8

This is why people have never called the knowledge coming from the senses 'light,'[35] even if the knowledge it gives is sometimes very sure. Only knowledge in the thoughts coming from the nous is given this name. In fact, we do not see any being gifted with reasoning activity[36] who lacks a noetic light. The angels are like an immaterial and incorporeal fire. What is that if not a noetic light? Nous, when it sees itself, sees as if by that light. Again, what is it that it sees, if not the noetic light?

God himself, who surpasses all noetic light and transcends essence upon essence, is called 'fire' by the holy theologians. He possesses this mysterious and invisible character in himself, (like a faint image of what fire is among sensory things,) whenever there is no matter to receive the divine appearance. But when it acquires suitable matter that is undisguised, (for example, any purified noetic nature not bearing a veil of evil), then it appears as a noetic light in the way we have shown. We will show this again in reference to the saints, who submit to and contemplate the radiance of God.

3.9

Just as fire, if it is hidden by opaque material, may give heat without light, as long as it is covered by the veil of evil passions, the nous too can receive knowledge but not light. Nous is not only contemplated[37] by nous as a light, the last light seen in this way, but at the same time it is contemplation itself, like an eye in the inmost centre of the psyche.[38] It is said, in fact, that: *"The nous is joined to the psyche as its organ of sight."* Just as the eye of the senses cannot act unless it is illumined by an exterior light, so the nous cannot act as the organ of noetic sense[39] and cannot initiate action unless the divine light illumines it.

Just as the eye, when it acts, itself becomes light, confuses itself with the light, and first sees this same light flooding onto the objects which it sees, in the same way the nous, when it wakes its noetic sensibility to activity, is itself entirely like light. Then it is in the light, and with the aid of the light it sees the light clearly, in a way that is not only superior to the bodily senses, but also to everything we know, and, simply, superior to all created things.

For it is God who is seen by those who have purified their hearts, according to the beatitude of the Lord who makes no mistake. And: *"God is light,"* according to the most theological of the words of John, the son of thunder. He makes His home in them, and shows Himself to those who love Him and are loved by Him, according to the promise that He gave them.[40]

He shows Himself to the purified nous as in a mirror, while all the while He Himself remains invisible. This is how an image appears in a mirror: it appears [in reflection], while all the while remaining invisible in itself. It is almost impossible to see at the same time both the image reflected in the mirror and the object which the mirror reflects.

3.10

This is how God appears now to those who have been purified in love, but one day, it is said, He will appear to them 'face to face.'[41] Those who do not believe that God appears now as a light beyond light, because they have no appreciation of things noetic and do not see them, and those who believe that unaided reason can contemplate, are like blind people who only receive the warmth of the sun and do not believe those who also see its rays. And if these blind people undertake to give lessons to those who see, saying to them that the sun, the most luminous of the objects of the senses, is not a light, those who possess sensitive eyes can only laugh.

These people of whom you speak are in rather the same situation in relation to the *'Sun of righteousness,'*[42] which is above the cosmos.[43] Not only those who truly possess noetic vision, but even those who have confidence in these visionaries, will bemoan the fate of such people.

God, even though He transcends all things and is incomprehensible and indescribable, consents in an excess of goodness towards us to allow our nous to participate in, and become invisibly visible in, His indivisible power beyond essence.[44] But people like these do not respond with love to this visible and purely noetic love. More than this, they do not wish to follow the saints who, in their love towards men, lead them with words towards that light. Instead, full of pretentiousness, they begin to draw to them those who have confidence in the saints, and to make companions of them.

According to Gregory the Theologian, then *"they will see as fire Him whom they did not recognise as light,"*[45] and in Whom they have not had faith. But this fire is full of darkness: it is even identical with the darkness which threatens us; it is from that which *"is prepared for the devil and his angels,"* in the words of the Lord.[46] If it was prepared for evil angels who lack the ability to sense, this means it is not simply a darkness of the senses. It is not just ignorance, for those who today allow themselves to be convinced by the heirs of this darkness will be no more unaware of God than they are now. They will know him even better, for it is said that: *"All flesh confesses that Jesus Christ is the Lord, to the glory of God the Father."* [47] Amen.

But if this light, although it is not knowledge, nevertheless brings to us the mystical and indescribable knowledge of the mysteries of God. So this pledge, visible even now[48] to those who have purified their hearts, is not simple knowledge, but it corresponds to knowledge, because this light itself is intelligible and noetic, or rather it is spiritual: spiritually[49] present, and spiritually visible. It effectively transcends all knowledge and all virtue, and, entirely alone, will procure for Christians the perfection[50] accessible to them here below. This does not come from imitation, nor from reasoning[51] activity. It is the effect of revelation, and the grace of the Spirit.

3.11

This is the reason why the great Macarius, confirmed by the testimony of Symeon, the most pleasant interpreter to hear, told us: *"The divine apostle Paul has shown each psyche the perfect mystery of Christianity in a most precise and luminous way. This mystery is a ray of heavenly light, produced in a revelation of the power of the Spirit so that people will not believe that the illumination of the Spirit is simply the product of conceptual knowledge, and so that there is no risk that, by ignorance and carelessness, they might make a mistake about the perfect mystery of grace.*

"This is why he first put forward as evidence that everyone would recognise, the example of the glory of the Spirit shining round Moses' face. 'But in fact,' he said, 'if what is transient was glorious, what endures is even more glorious.'[52] *He spoke of it as a passing*

thing, because the glory shone round the mortal body of Moses. But he has showed that this immortal glory of the Spirit, which appeared in a revelation, and today shines on the immortal face[53] of the interior man, shines permanently for those who are worthy of it.

"He therefore says: 'All of us, that is to say all those who are born of the Spirit through perfect faith, all of us who contemplate the glory of the Lord with unveiled face, are transfigured into the same image, from glory to glory, just as in the Spirit by the Lord.' [54] *He said 'unveiled faces' when he was speaking about their psyches because, he said, when someone is converted* [55] *to the Lord, the veil is lifted. For the Lord is the Spirit. He has clearly shown by this that a veil of darkness has covered the psyche, a veil insinuated into the heart of humanity by Adam's transgression. But today, through the illumination of the Spirit, this veil has been removed from those psyches who truly believe and are worthy.*

"This is the reason for the coming of Christ."

3.12

Do you see, brother, how the perceptible illuminations that happened under the old law prefigured the illumination of the Spirit which occurs in the psyches of those who truly and effectively believe in Christ? People who speak of it as if they are describing sensible and symbolic appearances should be led by this to faith and to the search for Christ. That is how they should seek.

But, to the contrary, such people seek by any means to evoke unbelief in others who believe, and even, if possible, in those who have received grace in a visible way and thanks to that possess indestructible knowledge. They have the audacity and the folly to teach their new ideas to those whom God, through His manifestations and His indescribable energies, has initiated into the mysteries. They do not allow themselves even to be moved by the great Paul when he says: *"The spiritual man judges everything, but is not himself judged by anyone, for he has the nous of Christ:*[56] *For who hath known the nous of the Lord, that he may instruct him?"* Does this say that he makes the things of the Spirit form the basis of his faith simply by

thinking his own thoughts? Someone who has faith in his own reasoning and the problems which it poses, who believes he can discover all truth by making distinctions, syllogisms and logical analyses, can neither know the things of the spiritual man directly, nor
believe in them. He is a psychic man, and: *"The psychic man,"* said
Paul, *"does not receive the things of the Spirit."*[57] Nor can he do so.
Simply by logic, then, how could someone who is ignorant, a man
without faith, make these things known to other men, and how would
he make them worthy of faith?

This means that if someone who is without hesychia and noetic
watchfulness, and who has no experience of these things, which occur spiritually and mysteriously, teaches about watchfulness, then
he is conforming himself to his own reasoning, and seeking to show
in words the Good which transcends all words, such a one has clearly
fallen into the final folly. He has been driven mad in his wisdom.[58]
In an insane way, he has set his mind to use natural knowledge to
observe the supernatural. He uses natural reason and carnal philosophy to examine and show *"the depths of God"* which can only be
known through the Spirit,[59] and the gifts of the Spirit, which can
only be known to those who are spiritual and possess the nous of
Christ.[60] In his folly, he will even succeed in being God's enemy by
misrepresenting the action and grace of the good Spirit - O misery -
as did Beliar in opposing himself *"to those who have received the
Spirit from God, so that they know the things which God has given
us by his grace."*[61] He will inherit misfortune for the harm he causes
to those who listen to him: what the prophet calls the misfortune due
to him who gives his brother the dregs of the wine to drink.[62]

3.13

Those who can judge everything, that is to say, the spiritual men, for
according to the Apostle *"the spiritual man judges all things,"* [63]
should bring under their authority those who cannot judge, so that
this judgement may permit them to know their own personality firmly.
But to the contrary, to their own loss and that of their disciples, these
people try to judge and correct spiritual men who are judged by no-

body. (*"The spiritual man,"* says the Apostle, *"is judged by no-body."*[64]) For they say that nobody can have a part in perfection and sanctity who does not possess a true opinion about created things. They then say that it is not possible to acquire this except by the methods of distinction, reasoning and logical analysis. Anybody who wishes to enjoy perfection and sanctity must necessarily receive the teaching of worldly education and learn their methods of distinction, reasoning and analysis. This is the conclusion to which they wish to lead us!

By this aim, they seek to make active once again the wisdom which has been abolished once for all time. Yet if they would come, in all humility, to those who can *"judge all things,"* wishing to learn the truth, they would hear one-another say that their own doctrine comes from Hellenic thought. This is identified with the heresy of the Stoics and the Pythagoreans, who claim that experimental knowledge from the study of the sciences is the aim of contemplation.

As for us, we believe that the true doctrine is not what is known through words and arguments, but what is demonstrated in people's works and lives. That is not only the truth, but the only certain and immutable truth.

"Every word," it is said, *"argues with some other word."* But what word can argue with life? [65] We even think that it is impossible to know yourself by the methods of distinction, argument and analysis unless you free your nous from pride and evil by laborious repentance[66] and active asceticism. Someone who has not worked on his nous by these means will not even know his own poverty in the domain of knowledge. So this is a practical way to begin to obtain self-knowledge.

3.14

A judicious man will not condemn ignorance in general, and we do not believe that all knowledge should be regarded as good, so why should we consider knowledge as the goal which determines all our activity? *"Truth,"* says the great Basil, *"has two aspects. There is one which it is absolutely necessary to possess and to communicate to others, as it contributes to our salvation. But as to the earth and the sea, the sky, and all that is in them, even if we do not know the truth about these things, nothing will prevent us from acquiring the promised beatitude."* [67] The goal before us is God's promise of good things to come: adoption, deification, revelation, the possession and enjoyment of heavenly treasures.

As to the knowledge which comes from worldly education, we know that it shares the fate of the present age. For if sensory language will reveal reality in the age to come, the wise men of this age will become heirs to the kingdom of heaven. But according to the true philosopher, Maximos: *"If it is the purity of the psyche which sees, then those sages will be far from the knowledge of God."* Why do we need knowledge which does not bring us closer to God? Can we possibly acquire perfection and holiness with it?

3.15

I will set aside the other opinions of these pretentious people who are mistaken to the point of giving a false interpretation of the Scriptures of the Spirit. Through this they have turned themselves against spiritual works and spiritual men. I will only add what relates to the subject of the present treatise. They say, in effect, that God is invisible and incomprehensible: *"No man hath seen God at any time; the only begotten Son, which is in the bosom of the Father, he hath declared him."* [68]

And they say, *"How then are not those who claim to see God as a noetic light in themselves obviously deluded?"* Any one of these men whom they attack can refute them with the Word, the only Son of God, Who said: *"Those who have a pure heart will see God."* [69] And *"I will make Myself known to them, having made my home in them with my Father."* [70] But immediately they will reply that their contemplation is knowledge, without noticing that they are contradicting themselves. In fact, the divine is not only invisible but also incomprehensible. So those who teach that because God is invisible, the noetic vision of God in the light is the fruit of a wandering imagination and daemonic activity, should also reject all knowledge described in similar language because God is incomprehensible.

We prefer not to reply to them about knowledge, for they are in agreement with us even if they do not understand what they say. In fact, there is knowledge about God and His doctrines, a contemplation which we call theology. On the one hand, the use and the natural movement of the powers of the psyche and the members of the body produce a transformation of the images in our thoughts.[71] But this is not the dawn of the perfect beauty of the noble state which comes to us from above. It is not the supernatural union with the most resplendent light, which is the one source of sure theology, the effect of which is to organise the interior power of psyche and body, and to make them move in conformity with nature. In rejecting this, they have rejected all virtue and all truth.

3.16

What this means is that no contemplation that is very indescribable and very high belongs in any way to the domain of that knowledge they describe. The contemplation of God [that they describe] does not exist, because God is invisible, as we have learned when we have been with those who participate in true contemplation. But we will put the following question to these people: do you think that the Holy Spirit does not see what concerns God? For it is He Who *"searches out the deep things of God."* [72]

If someone pretended to see the pure light without the help of the Holy Spirit, you would be right to confront him, and to say to him: *"How could one see the invisible?"*

But if a man rejects the spirit of the world, which the fathers call *"the noetic darkness that oppresses unpurified hearts:"* If he rejects that, purifies himself of all his self-will, keeps himself apart from all human tradition which even slightly weakens his enthusiasm for accomplishing his task, even though this tradition seems good:

If, like the great Basil, he gathers the powers of his psyche together properly, and stabilises the eye of his heart[73] in watchfulness:

If he then lives meditating in his nous on what is true to nature and what pleases God, and:

If, on the other hand, he transcends himself and receives into himself *"the Spirit which comes from God,"* and which *"knows the things of God just as the spirit of man knows what is within a man:"* [74]

If he receives this Spirit, according to the preaching of the great Paul, *"in order to know the things which God has given him mystically by His grace;"* that *"which eye has not seen, which ear has not heard, and which has never arisen in the heart of man,"* [75] then how would this man not see the invisible light of the Spirit? And how, even if it was the object of his vision, would this light not remain invisible, inaudible, and incomprehensible in itself?

Those who look see what *"eye has not seen, ear has not heard, and which has never arisen in the heart of man!"* Such men, in fact, receive spiritual eyes and possess the Nous of Christ.[76] Thus they can see the Invisible and can noetically think[77] of the Incomprehensible, for it is not invisible to them, but only to those who think and see only with their natural and created eyes and thoughts. As for those to whom God has adapted Himself as a faculty which directs[78] them, in this case how would He not communicate the contemplation of His grace to them in a way that they can perceive?

3.17

How would The Psalmist not be applying the theological language of *The Song Of Songs* when he sings the praises of the spiritual power in their eyes? *"See that you are beautiful,"* he says to Him, *"you who are close to me; your eyes are like the eyes of doves."* [79] And they, when they perceive the beauty of the noetic Betrothed, praise Him abundantly in the same terms. When they clearly see the beauty of God in His Betrothed for the first time, the initiates know what this dove is which is in the eyes of the Betrothed.[80] He describes this benevolent beauty in detail for those who listen to him in faith. Just as when the radiance in the eyes, when it is united to the radiance of the sun, acts as light, and so sees sensory things, in the same way the nous, having become *"one Spirit with the Lord,"* sees spiritual things clearly.[81]

But even there, the Master remains invisible in a different way, a way truly superior to those who make him invisible by the earth-bound thoughts of those who set out to contradict spiritual men. Nobody has ever seen the fullness of this beauty, which is why, according to Gregory of Nyssa, *"no eye has seen it, not even that which watches continually."*[82]   In fact, the eye does not see that fullness as it really is, except to the measure that it is made receptive by the power of the divine Spirit. Beside the incomprehensibility, what is most divine and extraordinary is that, if they understand it, they understand it in an incomprehensible way. Those who see, in fact, do not know what allows them to see, to hear, and to be initiated into a knowledge of the future, or to experience things eternal, for the Spirit by which they see it is incomprehensible.

As the great Dionysius said, *"The union of someone who has been divinised, to the light which comes from above, occurs when all noetic activity ceases."*[83]   It is not the product of a cause, nor is it just a relationship, for these are both results of activity in the nous, while this union occurs as a result of interior separation. But it is not itself separation,[84] for if it was simply separation, it would depend on us, and that is like the doctrine of the Messalians, that: *"They go up to the hidden mysteries of God whenever they wish,"* as Saint Isaac[85] said about them.

So contemplation is not simply separation or negation, it is a union and a divinisation which occurs, mystically and inexpressibly by the grace of God, after we have separated ourselves from all that has come from below to write on[86] the nous. In fact, it happens after the cessation of all noetic activity. This is more than mere separation, and the inner separation is no more than the sign of that cessation. This is why every believer should consider God as separate from all His creatures, for the cessation of all noetic activity and the resulting union with the light from on high is an objective state, and part of the accomplishment of divinisation. It happens only to those who have purified their hearts and received grace.

And what may I say of this union, when the brief vision itself appears only to chosen disciples, washed clean of all perception in sense or nous.

They are admitted to true vision because they have ceased to see, and they are clothed with supernatural senses because they submit without knowing.

But we will show further on, with the help of God, that they have seen this vision, and that, properly speaking, the organ of their vision was neither the senses nor the nous.

3.18

Do you see now that in place of the nous, eyes, and ears, they acquire the incomprehensible Spirit? It is through Him that they see, hear and understand. For if all their noetic activity has come to rest, how could the angels and men like angels see God except by the power of the Spirit? This is why their vision is not sensory. They do not receive it by the senses. Nor is it an act of noetic perception, since they do not find it in thoughts, nor in the knowledge[87] that comes from them. They only discover it after all noetic activity ceases. So it is not the product of either imagination[88] or discursive reason,[89] neither is it an opinion,[90] nor a conclusion reached by syllogistic argument. On the other hand, the nous does not acquire this simply by raising itself up by means of negation.

According to the teaching of the fathers, every divine command and every sacred law has as its end purity of heart. Every mode and aspect of prayer is crowned by pure prayer. Every thought[91] which strives from below towards Him Who is transcendent and separate from the world, comes to a halt once it has gone beyond all creatures. Yet it is false to say that beyond the accomplishment of the divine commandments there is nothing but purity of heart. There are other things, many other things. There is the pledge of things promised in this age. There are also the blessings of the age to come, visible and accessible through this purity of heart. Then, beyond prayer, there is the vision that cannot be spoken of, the ecstasy in the vision, and the hidden mysteries.

Similarly, beyond abstraction from created things, or rather after the cessation - which happens within us not only in words, but in reality - there remains an unknowing which is more than knowledge. There is a cloud, but it is more than radiance, and, as the great Dionysius says,[92] it is in this dazzling darkness[93] that divine things are given to the saints.

Thus the most perfect contemplation of God and divine things is not simply interior abstraction. Beyond this abstraction there is a participation in things divine, more a gift and a possession than a process of abstraction. These possessions and gifts cannot be spoken of. If someone says anything about them, they must have recourse to images and analogies - not because these things are seen only as images and analogies, but because we cannot show what we have seen in any other way. When we talk about things that are indescribable, we must describe them in an imaginative way. Then those who do not lend a pious ear to it consider that this knowledge which surpasses all wisdom is simply foolishness. They trample the noetic pearls underfoot with their criticisms.[94] As far as is possible with words, they also strive to destroy those who have shown them these pearls.

3.19

As I have said, it is because of their love of men that the saints say as much as they possibly can about things that cannot be described. They reject the error of those who in their ignorance imagine that beyond abstraction from created things there remains only total inaction, not an inaction that transcends all activity. But, I repeat, these things remain impossible to describe by their very nature. This is why the great Dionysius says that after abstraction from created things, there is no word, but *"an absence of words."* [95] He also says, *"After every ascent we will be united with the Inexpressible."* [96] But despite the fact that it is also inexpressible, negation alone is not enough to enable the nous to attain things that are beyond the nous.

Ascent by negation is in fact merely a noetic understanding of things that appear to be different from God. It employs an image to represent inexpressible contemplation as well as the accomplishment [97] of the nous in that contemplation. It is not itself that accomplishment. But those who, like the angels, have been united to that light, sing of this using the image of total abstraction. A mystical union with the light beyond essence teaches them that this light transcends all things. Moreover, those judged worthy to receive the mystery, who have a faithful and prudent ear around these initiates, can also sing of the divine and incomprehensible light that comes when we are abstracted from all things.[98] But they can only unite themselves to it and see it if they have purified themselves by taking care to fulfil the commandments, and by consecrating their nous to pure and immaterial prayer, thus receiving the supernatural power of contemplation.

3.20

What then shall we call this power which is neither sensory nor noetic activity? How else except by using the expression of Solomon, who was wiser than all who went before him and said that it is, *"a sensation that is both noetic and divine."* [99]

By combining those two adjectives, he urges his hearer to consider it neither as solely a sensation nor as simply a noetic activity, for neither is the activity of the nous a sensation, nor is that of the senses a noetic activity. The noetic sense is thus different from both. Following the great Dionysius, we should perhaps call it 'union,' and not 'knowledge.' *"We should realise,"* he says, *"that our nous possesses both a noetic power, which permits it to see noetic things, and also a power of union which surpasses the nature of the nous and allies it to that which transcends it."*[100] And again: *"The noetic powers, as well as the senses, become superfluous when the psyche becomes deiform, abandoning itself to the rays of the inaccessible light in an unknowing union of sightless comprehension."*[101]

In this union, as St. Maximos, so rich in things divine, puts it: *"In beholding the light of the hidden glory which cannot be put into words, the saints too, like the celestial powers, become capable of receiving the blessed purity."*

3.21

We do not think that these great men have in mind the ascent by the negative way! For the latter lies within the powers of anyone who wants it, but it does not transform the psyche to give it an angelic dignity. It frees the thoughts from the influence of other created things, but it cannot by itself effect union with transcendent things.

Purity of the passionate part of the psyche, dispassion effectively liberates the nous from all things. It is then united through prayer to the grace of the Spirit. This enables it to enjoy the divine radiance, so that the nous acquires an angelic and godlike form.

This is why the fathers, since the time of Dionysius the Great, called this state *"spiritual sensation,"* a phrase which agrees most with that mystical and hidden contemplation, and describes it best. But at such times, in fact, man truly sees neither by the nous, nor by the body, but by the Spirit. Then he at once knows, about what he sees, that supernaturally he sees a light that is beyond light. Yet at that moment he does not know what organ allows him to see this light, nor can he discover the nature of that organ, for he cannot follow the traces of the Spirit. This was what Paul said when he heard the unspeakable words and saw invisible things. In fact he said: *"I know not whether I saw out of the body or in the body."* [102] In other words, he did not know whether it was his nous or his body which saw.

Such a person does not see by sense perception, but his vision was as clear as that which permits the senses to perceive sensory things, and even clearer. He saw by going out of himself, and was ravished beyond all objects, and all objective thought, by the indescribable sweetness of his vision.

Under the influence of this ecstasy, he forgot prayer to God. It is this of which St. Isaac speaks, confirming the great and divine Gregory: *"Prayer is the purification of the nous which is alone with the fright[103] produced by the light of the Holy Trinity."*

112

And again: *"Purity of nous is what allows the light of the Holy Trinity to shine at the moment of prayer. The nous then transcends prayer, and this state should not properly be called prayer, although it is a fruit of the pure prayer sent by the Holy Spirit. Then the nous no longer prays any definite prayer. It finds itself in ecstasy amidst incomprehensible realities. This is 'the ignorance that is higher than knowledge."* [104]

This most joyful reality ravished Paul and made his nous step back[105] from every created thing, so that he returned entirely into himself. This he beheld as a light - a light of revelation, although it did not reveal sensible bodies. It was a light with no limit either in depth, or in height, or to either side. He saw absolutely no limit to his vision, or to the light which shone on him, as if it were a sun infinitely brighter and greater than the universe.

He held himself at the centre of it, having become all eye.

His vision was something like this.

3.22

This is why the great Macarius says that this light is infinite and beyond the heavens.[106] Another saint, one of the most perfect, saw the whole universe contained in a single ray of this noetic sun[107] - even though he himself did not see the full nature and the measure of that light, seeing it only to the measure that he was able to make himself receptive. In this contemplation, in his union with this light beyond the nous, he did not learn its nature, but he did learn that it really exists, is supernatural, beyond all essence, and different from all created things. He learned too that its being is absolute and unique, and that it mysteriously comprehends all created things in itself.

This vision of the Infinite cannot permanently belong to any individual, nor to all men together. He who does not see [this light] will understand that he himself is unable to see because he is not perfectly adapted to the Spirit by complete purification. It is not the Object of vision that disappears. When the vision comes down to him, the seer knows with certainty that it is the light. Although he still sees this in

113

quite an obscure way, he knows it surely by the passionless joyfulness of the vision that springs in him, by the calm that he feels in his nous, and by the fire of love that begins to burn in him.

In an analogous way, he always makes progress in the practices agreeable to God, in his resistance to everything else, in his application to prayer, and in the total elevation of his psyche towards God, at the same time he experiences ever more resplendent contemplation. He then understands that his vision is infinite because it is The Infinite, and because he cannot see the end of its radiance. Even more, he sees how feeble is his own capacity to receive the light.

3.23

But such a man does not consider that the vision of which he has been made worthy is simply the nature of God. Just as the embodied psyche[108] communicates its life to the living body, (and we call this life 'psyche,' all-the-while knowing that the psyche which is in us, and which communicates life to us, is distinct from that life), so God, Who dwells in the God-bearing psyche, communicates light to it. However, the union of God, the cause of all, with those who are worthy, transcends that light. God, while remaining entirely in Himself, dwells entirely in us by His power that transcends the essential. He does not communicate His nature to us, but His own glory and splendour.

This light is thus divine, and the saints rightly call it 'divinity' because it is the source of deification. So it is not only 'divinity' but 'deification-itself,'[109] and the rule of God. It appears as distinction and multiplicity in the one God, but it is no less He Who is the Divine Principle, more-than-God and more-than-Principle. This is the One in the one Divinity. This is why it is the Divine Principle, more-than-God and more-than-Principle, since God is the Existence of this Divinity, as the doctors of the Church have taught, following the great Areopagite Dionysius. They too called the deifying gift that comes from God 'divinity.' So when Gaius asked Dionysius how God could be beyond thearchy, he replied in his letter: *"If you think of the reality of the Gift which deifies us as 'divinity', and if this Gift is the cause of deification, He Who is above all causes is*

also above what you call 'divinity.' "Which things also we speak,
not in the words which man's wisdom teacheth, but which the Holy
Ghost teacheth; comparing spiritual things with spiritual."[110]

So the fathers say that the divine grace of the light that is beyond
the senses is God. But God in his nature does not simply identify
Himself with this grace, because He is able not only to illumine and
deify the nous, but to bring every noetic essence out of non-being.

3.24

Do you see how those who see the light still think of it as invisible? Those most expert in the worldly wisdom do no better.
Those who are elevated to that degree of contemplation know
that they see a light with their noetic sense. They know that this
light is God who, by his grace, makes those who participate in
the union mysteriously[111] luminous. And if you ask them how
they see the Invisible, they will answer you: *"not in the words*
which man's wisdom teaches, but through those by which the
Holy Spirit teaches."[112] In fact, they lack nothing, they do not
need human wisdom, since they possess the teaching of the Spirit,
and *"that makes them glorious"* like the Apostle.

This is because they *"behaved in the world with simplicity, purity,*
and Godly sincerity, not with fleshly wisdom."[113] They will answer
you piously that: *"Things divine, O man, are not in the least limited*
by our knowledge. On the contrary, many things of which we are
ignorant have their origin in God. According to the same Apostle, it
is by comparing the spiritual to the spiritual[114] *in this way that we*
establish that the grace of the New Covenant is in agreement with
the Old." The Apostle called this demonstration from the old covenant 'comparison,' for after having 'established' the new things in
this way, we can also show that the gifts of grace are superior to
those of the law.

115

And if you question them again, asking: *"Why do you say that prayer sounds mystically in your inner heart, and that it is this which sets your heart in motion?"* They will then cite as authority the earthquake which Elias felt, which preceded the actual noetic appearance of God.[115] They will also refer to the sounding of the stomach described in Isaiah.[116] And if you then ask them why prayer produces warmth in us, they will speak of the fire which the same Elias describes as a sign of God before His appearance, a sign that will change again, becoming like a light breeze when it touches the divine radiance, indicating that it really is the Invisible who is revealed by it.

They will also speak of Elias, who appears and really was like a fire when he ascended in his body in a chariot of fire.[117] They will also speak of the other prophet whose entrails were burned as if by fire. The Word of God had become fire in him?[118] And if you wish to ask other questions about what happens indescribably within them, they will tell you about things very similar to those we have spoken of already, things equally Spiritual. They will say always and to everyone: *"Have you not heard, man, that a man has eaten the bread of angels?"*[119] *"Did you not hear the Lord say that he will give the Holy Spirit to those who ask Him night and day?"*[120]

What is the bread of angels? Is it not the divine light beyond the heavens? According to the great Dionysius, the nous unites to this, directly or by transmission,[121] in a way that transcends the nous? God gave a promise of this illumination to men by sending manna from above for forty years. Christ accomplished it by sending the illumination of the Spirit to those who firmly believe in Him and who make their faith manifest in their works, by offering them his body as the illuminator in food. This last is a pledge of the unspoken communion with Jesus still to come.

So there is nothing astonishing in the fact that these events of the Old Testament prefigured other graces of Christ. Do you see, then, that these symbolic illuminations lead to the appearance of a noetic illumination, and of mysteries other than knowledge?

But since those who reject the divine light of grace say, as you tell us, that the light which appeared on Tabor was a light perceptible by the senses, we will ask them whether they consider the light which then shone on the chosen disciples at Tabor as Godlike? Because if they do not consider it theological, Peter will convince them of their mistake. According to Mark, he kept vigil on the mountain and saw the glory of Christ,[122] and in the second of his epistles he himself writes that *"while he was with Him on the holy mountain, he had contemplated His majesty."*[123] It is the interpretation of the Gospel preaching, given quite clearly by the one with the golden tongue,[124] that will clearly close their mouths. He said: *"The Lord appeared brighter, His body retaining its shape, but the Divinity showing its radiance."* Their mouths were finally closed by Dionysius the Great, who clearly calls the event *"theophany, and even the vision of God."* In addition, Gregory, surnamed the Theologian, says that *"the Divinity manifested to the disciples on the mountain was a light."*[125] Many others have said the same. Finally, Symeon, who celebrated the lives of nearly all the saints in his beautiful language, wrote that the Theologian particularly loved by Christ *"saw the very Divinity of the Word unveiled"*[126] on the mountain.

But if these people, consistent with the truth and its interpreters, called this manifested light 'Divine light,' and also, the 'light of God,' they will necessarily agree to saying that the most perfect vision of God is a light. This is why Moses too saw it in that way, as did almost all the prophets, particularly those to whom He appeared while they were awake and not while they slept. But so be it: all the sacred visions of the prophets had a symbolic character, and those who contradict us want it so.

Yet the vision revealed to the apostles on Tabor was not a symbolic light that appears then disappears. In fact, it has the value of the second coming of Christ which is to come. This same light will eternally illumine those who become worthy of it in the Age Without End, as the divine Dionysius says. Basil the Great speaks of it as the prelude to the Second Coming, and the Lord in the Gospels calls it *"the Kingdom of God."* [127]

3.27

Why then do they oppose what is said about the saints who indescribably see God as a light, when that vision today, just as much as in the age to come, is like a light? Is it because these saints do not say that this light is a light of the senses, but call it 'noetic,' as Solomon called the Holy Spirit? And it is these same people who malign them, saying that they pretend to gaze at a sensory light during prayer! They also oppose everyone who admits [that there is] some sensory element in the holy gifts! How then - forgetting themselves - can they heap scorn on those who say that the divine light is not sensory? Do you see their inconsistency and their inconstancy? They seem eager to criticise, but not to see the good!

But what would they reply, then, these infallible interpreters of old and new appearances of the light,[128] if it happened that an animal without reason was then present on the mountain? Would it have perceived this radiance that is more luminous than the sun? I do not think so. It is not written that the herds felt the Glory of The Lord that illumined the shepherds at the time of Christ's birth.[129] So how could this light be sensory if the present and open eyes of the unreasoning animals - which see sensory things in the normal way - do not see it when it illumines them!

So if it is the eyes of human senses which saw it, they saw it only in as much as they are different from eyes without reason. In what way would they be different? Only in one thing. It is the nous which sees with human eyes. It is not a matter of a sensory faculty, or beings without reason would also have been able to see it. Was it a noetic faculty perceiving the light through the senses? No, it was not a faculty of this kind, otherwise everyone, especially those in the countryside around, would have seen a radiance brighter than the

118

sun. So if it was not this faculty which permitted the apostles to see the light, it was not, properly speaking, a light of the senses.

Another thing, nothing known through the senses is eternal, but the light of the Divinity, often called *the glory of God,* has neither beginning nor end.

So it is not sensory.

3.28

If it is not sensory, although the apostles were judged worthy of perceiving it with their eyes, it was [known] through another power than that of the senses. That is why the radiance of Jesus' face was unspeakable, unapproachable, and timeless - because it acted through an indescribable reality. This is why they say that this radiance was not, properly speaking, accessible to the senses. It is the same as that light which is the place of saints hereafter, when they go to receive their allotted place in heaven. There is a light there of which this radiance is no more than a foretaste, a light here below which is accorded to the saints like a pledge. But if that is called 'light,' and sometimes appears in a strange way to become accessible to the senses, it is nevertheless part of a reality which transcends the nous itself, and the names which are given to it are extended from their ordinary meanings.

How, then, could it properly be called sensory?

Otherwise, when we pray for the deceased, why do we cry continually as we call on the thearchic Goodness: *"Keep their psyches in a place of light."* What need have these psyches of a sensory light, and why would they be afflicted by the darkness that was the opposite of this light, if it was simply a sensory darkness? Do you see that none of these things properly belong to the domain of the senses? We also showed earlier on, when we mentioned the dark fire prepared for the race of daemons, that this is also not simply a matter of ignorance or knowledge.

It was therefore not necessary to make statements about the indescribable and luminous appearance of Jesus on Tabor that depend on the lower forms of reasoning, that is, on human reasoning and unstable thoughts. But it was necessary to be obedient to the voice of the fathers and wait for the exact knowledge that comes from experience in purity of heart. This last knowledge actually accomplishes the union with this light; it mystically tells those who find it that this light cannot be compared to any being, as it transcends all created things.

For how can we regard as sensory something that transcends all created things?

How could the radiance of God be a creature?

So this light is certainly not sensory.

3.29

The great Macarius says: *"When the psyche, like the prodigal son, returns to God, his Master and his Father, in fear, love, and shame, God receives it without thinking of its transgressions and clothes it in a robe of glory, a robe of the light of Christ."*[130] Is there another glory and another light of Christ beyond that seen by Peter when, fully awake, *"he was with Him on the holy mountain?"* [131] How could it become a garment for the psyche if it belongs to the domain of the senses? The same theologian said elsewhere: *"This light is beyond heaven."*[132]

Could something sensory be 'beyond heaven?'

Elsewhere he says: *"The Lord made the mixture of human nature that was assumed by Him sit on the right hand of the divine majesty in the heavens,*[133] *in a fullness of glory visible not only on His face, as with Moses, but on his whole body."* If nobody perceives this light, does it shine in vain? Yes, if the light is sensory. Is it not actually the food of the spirits, of angels, and of the just? This is why, when we pray for the dead, we ask Christ to *"place their psyches where they are watched over by the light of His face."*[134] How could these psyches be joyful, and more, how could they live in the middle of a light which shone in a sensory way? The great Basil says on his part that, when the Master appears in the flesh, the pure in heart will *"see eternally this power whose radiance comes from the beloved Body."*

How could a light which is seen only in purity of heart be seen by the senses? According to Cosmas, the divine musician, *"Christ on the mountain appeared as infinite light."*

How could a sensory light be infinite?

3.30

And Stephen, who was the first after Christ to bear witness to Christ, *"turning his eyes upwards, sees the heavens open and the glory of God, and Christ standing on the right hand of God."* [135] Is it then possible to reach with our senses as far as realities beyond the heavens? Yet this man saw them while remaining here on earth. What is even more admirable was that he not only saw Christ, but also His Father. How could he have seen that the Son was on His right, if he had not also seen the Father?

The invisible allows itself to be seen by those whose hearts are purified, but by an indescribable power in a manner which is neither sensible, nor noetic, nor apophatic, for the sublime majesty and the glory of the Father cannot be in any way accessible to the senses.

On the other hand, the position on the right was symbolic, although the vision was not. Although the position itself was only a symbol [standing] for Him Who is fixed and immutable, like the absolutely unchangeable permanence of the divine nature, yet Stephen saw it in an indescribable way. For the position to the right was not a trick by the Only Begotten, intended to show a different reality, but by being always to the right of the Father, He clearly wanted to show His own glory to someone who was still in the flesh but had surrendered his very psyche for that glory.

Cessation does not make us either see or understand, yet Stephen saw the glory of God. And if this was a noetic vision, or if it was the result of deduction or analogy, that would mean that we too should be able to see as he saw. We too are able to represent the God become man by analogy – showing Him standing or seated in heaven on the right of the divine Majesty. But why was this vision not previously and always in the nous of the disciple of the Evangelist? Why did he grasp it only at that exact moment? *"Behold,"* he said, *"I see the heavens opened and the Son of Man standing on the right hand of God."* [136] What need had he to *"turn his eyes to heaven,"* and for heaven to *"open,"* if this vision had been no more than knowledge obtained noetically? Yet in what way did the First Martyr have this vision if he saw it neither noetically, nor with the senses, nor by negation: if he conceived these divine things neither by deduction nor by analogy? I will dare to tell you: spiritually! This is what I have said about those who see the pure light through revelation, as so many fathers have said before me.

The divine Luke also teaches this, saying: *"Stephen, full of faith and the Holy Spirit, turning his eyes to heaven, saw the glory of God."* And you too, if you are full of faith and the Holy Spirit, will be able to contemplate spiritually things which are invisible to the nous. But if, on the other hand, you remain entirely empty of faith, you will not even believe those who give witness[137] that they have seen these things. But if you had even a small measure of faith, you would listen piously to those who would tell you - as far as possible from their experience - about things that are indescribable. You would not treat them as if they were at the level of things sensory or noetic, even if these terms are applied to them. You would not fight against the truth as if it were an error, nor would you reject the indescribable grace of God which has been given to us.

3.31

In fact, the fathers call this contemplation *'particularly true,'* for prayer communicates this activity to the heart. Related to it are the spiritual warmth and joy which come from it, and the comforting tears which grace gives us, for this is the cause of what is in fact acquired by the noetic sense. I say 'sense,' because the perception involved is manifest and clear, free from delusion[138] and imagination. In other words, the body also participates in a certain way in the grace which acts through the nous. It harmonises with it, and it too becomes sensitive to the hidden mystery which is occuring in the psyche. To any spectators seeing those who possess this grace from the outside, it then communicates through their senses a certain perception of what is being produced at that moment. This is also what made the face of Moses shine, for the interior radiance of his nous spread over his body; he shone so strongly that the brilliance of the light prevented those who saw him with their senses from fixing their eyes on him.[139]

This is how the sensible face of Stephen appeared like the face of an angel[140] Within him, in fact, his nous took on an angelic appearance because it imitated the angels and acquired what is proper to them, while uniting - either directly or by transmission - in an indescribable participation in the Light which transcends all things. This is also how Mary of Egypt, or rather Mary of Heaven, rose bodily into the air when praying, perceptibly and really changing her position, for as her nous rose, her body also rose and left the earth. It was seen as a flying body.[141]

3.32

Thus, when the psyche is transported and set in motion by irresistible love for the one object of Desire, the heart too begins to move, showing by spiritual leaps that it is in communion with grace. It is as if it is leaping up to meet the Lord when He comes with his Body in the clouds, as has been promised.[142] Thus, in unceasing prayer, when the noetic fire appears, when the noetic torch is lit, and when, through the heavenly fire of spiritual contemplation, the nous awakens its desire, then, in a strange way, the body too becomes bright and warm. To those who see it, according to the writer who described the spiritual ladder,[143] it appears to come from a furnace visible to the senses.

For myself, I believe that the sweat of Christ as He prayed[144] was also a sign of heat felt by the senses, and that this can only be communicated to the body in prolonged supplication to God. What will those people reply to that, those who claim that the origin of the heat produced by prayer is daemonic? Will they teach us to avoid vehenment, energetic and continuous prayer, lest the body receive heat proportional to the struggles of the psyche? Is this what they wish to prevent? Then they are teaching prayer that neither leads a man to God, nor to the imitation of God, and does not transform him to make him any better!

We know for ourselves that by voluntarily accepting the pain of asceticism we rid ourselves of the pleasures which, alas, we had previously preferred once we had broken the commandment. Then, during prayer, we taste with our noetic sense a divine joy unmixed with pain. The prophet who had experienced this joy which - O miracle - had transformed his body itself to make it accessible to the dispassionate and divine love, proclaimed before God: *"Your words are sweet to my palate, sweeter than honey to my mouth;"* [145] and also: *"My psyche shall be satisfied as with marrow and fatness; and my mouth shall praise thee with joyful lips:"* [146]

Through this, the possibilities of ascent that are laid out in the heart participate in the 'godlike happiness' and angelic 'pleasure' of what Dionysius the Great called the 'divinising visitation of the divine radiance.'

3.33

But the divinely purifying sorrow not only manifests in the psyches of spiritual wrestlers. It also passes into their bodies and into the senses in their bodies. The tears of sorrow poured out by those who feel this pain because of their sins are the obvious proof of this. Why then do we not receive the signs of divine joy according to the Spirit just as piously when they are manifested by the faltering senses of the body? Is this not why the Lord says that *"Blessed are they that mourn: for they shall be comforted."* [147] ... because they will receive

124

the joy that is the fruit of the Spirit? But the body also participates in this consolation in many different ways. Those who have experienced this know it. On the other hand, even those who see them from the outside observe the good character of these last, their sweet tears, their conversation full of grace to those who come to see them. As it is said in the Song of Songs:[148] *"the honey of bees flows from your mouth, O my spouse."*

In fact, it is not only the psyche which receives the promise of good things to come, but also the body, which runs the race of the Gospel with it. Those who do not admit this also deny that the body lives in the age to come.

And if it is true that one day the body will participate in these indescribable good things, even now it can participate in them according to its nature when God gives grace to the nous. For this reason we say that these gifts are received by the senses, but we add *"by the noetic senses,"* because these transcend the natural senses, since it is pre-eminently the nous which receives them. [This is] because our nous ascends as far as possible towards the First Nous and participates in It divinely, transforming itself and so transforming the body which is attached to it and making it more divine. In this way it shows and prefigures the absorption of the flesh by the Spirit in the age to come.

It is not the eyes of the body but the eyes of the psyche which receive the power of the Spirit that allows them to see these things. We therefore call this power 'noetic,'[149] even though it is above the nous.[150]

3.34

At the same time, we will warn those who listen to us against thinking that these indescribable spiritual activities are material or corporeal. But some people are truly the victims of this opinion. With their impure and sacrilegious ears, with their thoughts which neither know, nor believe, nor follow the words of the fathers, they have received the teaching of the holy with very little holiness! They have trampled it under foot and set themselves against those who explained it to them.

They have not believed the great Macarius. Perhaps they do not even know that he said: *"Spiritual things are not accessible to people without experience, but the communion of the Holy Spirit can be received by the holy and faithful psyche. The heavenly treasures of the Spirit are only manifest to those who receive them through experience, while the uninitiated cannot even imagine them."*[151]

His words on this subject are devout! Listen to them so that faith may reach you and you may be worthy to receive these treasures! It is then that the true experience of the eyes of your psyche will show you what good things and what mysteries Christian psyches can receive in communion here below.

But when you hear talk of the *'eyes of the psyche,'* which can actually experience the heavenly treasures, do not confuse these with 'reason.' This last, in fact, exercises its faculties just as well on the things of the senses as on things noetic. Think of this in the same way that you would think of a city you had not yet seen: you cannot experience it simply by thinking of it. So it is with things that concern God and things Divine; you do not experience them simply by thinking or talking about them.

If you do not possess gold in a perceptible way, if you do not hold it perceptibly in your two hands, if you do not see it with your sensible eyes, you do not grasp it, you do not see it and you do not possess it, even if the thought of gold passes through your head ten thousand times: the same is true of thinking ten thousand times of divine treasures. Without confirming the divine things by experience, and without seeing them with the noetic eyes which transcend reason, you see nothing, you have nothing, you do not truly possess any of the divine things.

I have spoken of 'noetic eyes,' because it is through these that the power of the Spirit acts, permitting them to see these things. Yet this holy vision of the very divine and more than luminous light transcends the noetic eyes themselves.

126

This is why the Lord did not call all his disciples to the spiritual vision which appeared on Tabor, which was indescribable and invisible to the faculties of sense, but only chosen disciples. The great Areopagite, Dionysius, said that in the age to come we will be illumined *"by the visible theophany of Christ, as were the disciples at the time of the Transfiguration. But we will participate in this noetic light with our nous, made dispassionate and immaterial, and we will be in communion with the union which transcends the nous by ever-more divine emulation of nous beyond the heavens."* [152]

But even then, we will not come to conceive that the light shining from the beloved Body is a sensory radiance, perceived by the senses without the power of a reasoning psyche. Indeed, only this last power can receive the power of the Spirit, which in its turn can contemplate the light of grace. The radiance which cannot be perceived by these organs cannot be perceived at-all. The saint has shown this himself to those who have a nous. In the age to come, he says, we will be illumined by this light in a time when there is no need either of light, nor of air, nor of anything belonging to the present life.

The God-inspired scriptures tell us that - according to the Apostle: *"Then, God will be all in all."* [153] Then we will have no need for sensory light. For if God is everything for us, the light too will be divine. How could it then be perceptible by sense in the true meaning of the term? The fact that he added *"while becoming ever more divine like the angels,"* and that we can speak of it in three ways,[154] shows that angels also receive this light.

If it were sensory, how could this be? How could a sensible light not be visible through the air? We would then see the light more or less distinctly, not as a measure of each individual's virtue and the purity resulting from that virtue, but as a measure of the purity of the air! *"The just will shine like the sun."* [155] So each of them would appear brighter or darker not in proportion to their good actions, but merely depending on the purity of the air around them! What is more; in this case the good things of the age to come would be ac-

127

cessible to the eyes of the senses, now and forever. [Everyone would see] those good things which not only has *"eye not seen and ear not heard,"* but also which *"have not entered into the heart of"*[156] man who tries to penetrate incomprehensible things by verbal reasoning.

If it is sensory, how could this light be invisible to sinners? Or, according to these people, would there be a barrier formed of shadows and cones, of conjunctions resulting in eclipses, and of cycles of light in various forms? Will we need the vain activity of astronomers in a life of ages without end?

3.36

But how will the bodily senses grasp a light which is not truly sensible? By the power of the all-powerful Spirit, the power by which the chosen apostles themselves saw it on Tabor, when it blazed out not only from the flesh which carries the Son within it, but also from the cloud which carries within it the Father of Christ.

It will be different in the age to come. Then, according to the Apostle, the body itself will be 'spiritual' and no longer 'psychic:' *"It is sown a psychic body,"* he said, *"It is resurrected a spiritual body."* [157]

It is precisely because it will be spiritual and will see in a spiritual way that it will perceive the divine radiance.

Today we can see that, in truth, we have a noetic psyche, which exists in its own right within that dense and mortal flesh. This clothes it, and drags it down, so that the psyche becomes entirely like the body, and open to illusion. This is why our nous is unaware of the noetic sense.

In the same way, in the very blessed existence of the age to come, in *"the sons of the resurrection,"*[158] who, according to the Gospel of Christ, will have received an angelic dignity, it will be the body which is as if hidden. With the victory of the nous, the body will become so subtle that it will no longer appear to be material, and it will no longer limit the activity of the nous. In this way, they will enjoy the divine light in their bodily senses.

And why have I only spoken of the relationship which will be established then between the body and the noetic nature?[159] Saint Maximos said: *"The psyche becomes God by participating in the divine grace after it has ceased all noetic and sensory activity, as well as having ceased from all the natural activities of the body; for the body is divinised at the same time, participating in the deification in the way appropriate to it. God alone appears then, in the psyche, and in the body, because their natural characteristics are overcome by the great abundance of glory."* [160]

So, as I said at the beginning, God is invisible to creatures, but is not invisible to Himself. But then - O miracle! - it is God who will look, not only through the psyche within us, but also through our body. This is why we will then see the divine and inaccessible light distinctly, even with our own bodily organs. This was the pledge and the prelude of God's munificence that awaits us in the future. Christ showed it indescribably to the apostles on Tabor. How then can we say that the radiance of the Divinity, which is beyond all words and all vision, is in the domain of the senses? Have you now understood that in the strict sense of the term the light which illumined the apostles on Tabor was not exactly sensible?

Nevertheless, since that light, which is divine and beyond all sense perceptions, has appeared to the eyes of the senses – and this did happen - those who contradict these spiritual men recognise this for themselves, and agree on this point with them as well as with us. But if the divine light is apparent to their bodily eyes, could it not appear to noetic eyes as well? Could the psyche be an evil thing, incapable of uniting itself to the Good and becoming aware of it? No audacious heretic has ever said this! Could it be a good thing, but the body a better thing? How, in fact, could the psyche not be inferior to the body, if the body can participate in and grasp the light of God when the psyche cannot do so? Since it is by the psyche's mediation that the body sees God in the light, and not the other way round, how could this material and mortal body be more akin to and more devoted to God than is the psyche?

But since the Transfiguration of the Lord on Tabor was a prelude of God's visible appearance in the Glory which is still to come, then, if the apostles had been judged worthy to contemplate it with the eyes of their bodies, why should those whose hearts have been purified today not see with the eyes of their psyches the prelude and pledge of this appearance in their nous?

But the Son of God, in His incomparable love for men, not only unites His divine hypostasis with our nature, in order to *"appear on earth and live among men,"* possessing a psyche-bearing body animated by a nous-bearing psyche. He also unites - O miracle of incomparable abundance - with the human hypostases themselves, mingling Himself with each one of His faithful in their communion with His holy Body. He then becomes one Body with us, making of us a temple for the whole Divinity. For in the very Body of Christ *"all the fullness of the Divinity lives bodily."*[161]

Why then should he not illumine by the divine ray of His Body - which is in those who communicate worthily with it, enlightening their psyches as He illumined even the bodies of the disciples on Tabor? At that time, His Body, the source of the light of grace, was not united to our bodies. It illumined from the outside those who approached worthily, and transmitted this illumination to the psyche through the medium of the eyes of the senses. But now that it is mingled in us and exists within us, it truly illumines the psyche from within.

3.39

What then? In the age to come will we not see the Invisible *"face to face,"* as it is written?[162] Those whose hearts have been purified receive the pledge and prelude of this now, and see the noetic and invisible formation within them through the medium of the senses. For the nous is of an immaterial nature. One could say that it is a light, and related to the First and sublime Light in which all things participate, although that Light transcends them all.

By turning entirely toward the true Light in immaterial, unceasing, and purified prayer, the nous ascends toward God Himself without turning back; when it transforms itself, acquiring an angelic dignity, illumined, like the angels, by the First Light itself. By participation, this appears as that of which the Archetype is cause, manifesting in itself the splendour of that hidden Beauty, its resplendent and unapproachable radiance.

David, the divine musician, noetically sensing that radiance in himself, rejoiced in it and taught that great and indescribable thing to the faithful: *"The glory of our God is upon us."*[163]

If we did not feel and see in ourselves the radiance of God, and if we too sought it only through distinctions, syllogisms and analyses, instead of believing the fathers in all simplicity of heart, then how could we tolerate it when somebody says that someone else possesses the radiance of God? So John has done well to show us in his *Revelation* that *"nobody can know what is written on the white stone which the victor receives from God, except him who receives it."* [164] It is not just that it is absolutely impossible for a man who does not possess the stone to know this. Unless he lends an ear in faith to those who have seen it, he will not even know of its existence.

Then, he will consider that true contemplation is blindness, not because it transcends sense and knowledge like a holy cloud, but because according to him it absolutely does not exist. And if, in his inexperience and lack of faith, he is wicked enough to cause slander; if he is full of empty thoughts, a shameless despiser of the most venerable fathers, he will not only announce that this thing does not exist, but even, in his daemonic imagination - O sorrow! - he will give false teaching about the divine radiance.

And as you say, brother, some people today have come to this!

3.40

And here is another pretext that they invoke: that God is invisible, while the devil simulates an *"angel of light."*[165] But they do not understand that truth existed before all simulations. This means that if the devil,

131

simulating what truly exists, simulates an angel of light, this is because there truly exists an angel of light, a good angel. As the angel of light, what light is it that he reveals? Is it not the light of God, of which he is an angel? God is the light and the angel of God is the angel of the light.

It is not said, in fact, that *"he simulates the angel which is light,"* but *"the angel of light."* If the wicked angel simulates only one kind of knowledge and virtue, we could understand by this that the illumination which comes to us from God only brings us knowledge and virtue. But since the evil angel also brings an imaginary light that is different from both virtue and knowledge, then there is truly a noetic light that is true and divine, and which is different from both virtue and knowledge. The imaginary light is the Evil one himself, a shadow who imitates the true light. The true light - God Himself - Who illumines the angels and those men who are the equal of the angels, is truly an indescribable light, He shows Himself as light, and it is He Who transforms into light those who have pure hearts.

So we call Him Light, not only because He overcame the darkness of ignorance, but also, according to Saint Maximos[166] and Gregory the Theologian,[167] because he illumines psyches. And you will understand clearly from Saint Nilus that this illumination is not only knowledge or virtue, but that it transcends all human virtue and all human knowledge: *"The nous united in itself,"* he says, *"no longer contemplates anything sensory, nor any form of thought, but only unveiled nouses and divine radiance. From these flow peace and joy."*

Do you see this contemplation, which goes beyond all works, all habits, and beyond every thought? Did you hear the person who said earlier that *"he saw his own nous clothed in a celestial colour,"*[168] and who now shows it to us, visibly illumined by the divine radiance? When he shows you the way that leads you to this blessed experience, and this vision, let yourself be convinced again by his teaching. *"Prayer which strives for attention,"* he says, *"will discover a prayer which is only found if we pursue it with vigilance. Those who have truly prayed, binding their nous to divine prayer, are illumined by the radiance of God."*[169] If you wish, you may ask the divine Maximos as well? *"He who has made his heart pure,"* he said, *"not only knows the causes of lesser and secondary things in relation to God, but he sees God himself."*[170]

Where are they, those who teach that wisdom which is worldly, and has been made foolish, not only obtains the knowledge of created things for us, but lifts us up towards God? It is said that *"When God has come to be present in the heart, He judges it good to write his own message there with the Spirit, as if on the Mosaic tablets."*[171]

Where are those who think that God cannot be received within our hearts, when Paul, in front of others, said that the law of grace will be received not on tablets of stone, but on tablets of flesh: written on our hearts?[172]

Similarly, the great Macarius said: *"The heart directs the whole organism, and when grace inherits the heart, it reigns over all the thoughts and all the members. In fact, it is there that the nous is found, with all the thoughts of the psyche. It is there that we must look there to see if grace has inscribed the laws of the Spirit."* [173]

So let us listen again to Maximos, who in purity illumined us with knowledge and with more than knowledge: *"The pure heart is one that has presented to God a nous completely empty of all forms, so that it is ready to be imprinted by the one sign by which God readily reveals himself."*[174]

Where then are those who maintain that God can be known only through the knowledge of created things, and who refuse to know and accept the evidence which results from union? Even after God said, through one of the God-bearing fathers: *"Do not enroll in the school of a man or a book, but that of My rays and My radiance within you?"*

How can a nous that is a blank[175] slate, marked only by the imprint of the divine signs, fail to be superior to knowledge that comes from created beings?

The imprinting of the nous by the divine and indescribable signs of the Spirit is very different from the apophatic theology which raises the reason[176] towards God. Theology is also far removed from the vision of God in the light. It is as different from intimate conversation with God as knowledge is different from possession. To say something about God is not equivalent to meeting God! To say something, we need words, words we can pronounce, and we also need skill. Unless we merely want to possess knowledge, neither using it ourselves nor communicating it to others, we also need various material and examples, drawn from the forms of this world, to provide syllogisms from which exact demonstrations can be contrived. All or most of this is collected by sight or hearing, and all drawn more or less from this world, so that the wise ones of this age can also use it without needing to purify their life and their psyche.

On the contrary, we cannot possess God within us unless we are purified by virtue to the point where we go out of ourselves. We cannot associate with God in purity - and immerse ourselves in light without mixture to the limit of the possibilities of human nature - unless we rid ourselves of passions, and, turning our back on sensations and all that is sensory, ascend above thoughts and reasoning and the knowledge they procure, to abandon ourselves entirely to the immaterial and noetic activity of prayer.

It is by finding the ignorance which surpasses all knowledge that we can fill ourselves with the resplendent beauty of the Spirit, and in this that we can invisibly contemplate the rewards of the nature of the immortal cosmos.

Do you understand, then, in what an abyss that much-vaunted intellectual philosophy is lost? Its basis is sensation, and its end consists of a knowledge of the different aspects of sensation, knowledge which can be found without inner purity, and which does not in itself purify anyone of passion? On the contrary, the origin of spiritual contemplation is the Good, and this is made firm by purity of life. It is also a true and authentic knowledge of created things and of reality, but it does not come from study. It appears with purity, and it is the only thing which can distinguish what is truly good and useful from what is not.

The end toward which spiritual contemplation leads is the promise of the age to come, the ignorance which surpasses all knowledge, the knowledge which surpasses every concept, and an inexpressible participation in a hidden vision, with a mystical and hidden contemplation and a taste of eternal Light.

3.43

If you hear and understand what I say to you, you will know that this is truly the light of the age to come. It is the very light which illumined the disciples at the Transfiguration of Christ, and today it illumines the nous that has been purified by virtue and prayer. Dionysius the Areopagite clearly stated that in the age to come the bodies of the saints are both adorned and enlightened by the light of Christ which appeared on Tabor.[177] As Macarius the Great says: *"The psyche united to the light of the heavenly image is then initiated, in its very existence,[178] into the knowledge of the mysteries, while on the great day of the Resurrection, the body will also be illumined by the same heavenly image of glory."*

He said *"in its substance"*[179] so that nobody will think that this illumination comes from knowledge and concepts. To put it differently, the substance of the spiritual man is composed of three parts; the grace of the heavenly Spirit, the reasoning psyche, and the terrestrial body. Hear him again: *"The deiform image of the Spirit which is now as if imprinted within us will then give to the body itself an externally deiform and heavenly character."* And then: *"God, reconciled with humanity, restores the psyche which has received the true faith in the joy of the lights of heaven while it is still in the body. He then illumines the noetic sense anew by the divine light of grace. Later, he will also clothe the body in glory."* [180]

Next, he says: *"Only someone who has received them through experience is aware, through the eyes of his psyche, with what good things and what mysteries Christian psyches can communicate here below. But at the time of the resurrection the body itself can receive* these good *things, and see them and possess them when it becomes Spirit itself."*[181] Is it not clear that this is the same divine light which the apostles saw on Tabor? That this, which purified psyches contemplate now, has the same [form of] existence as the good things in the age to come? This is why the great Basil said that the light shining on Tabor at the time of the Transfiguration was a prelude to the glory of Christ at the time of the second coming. He says this clearly enough: *"The divine power appears like a divine light seen through a pane of glass, illumining those who have purified the eyes of their heart, that is to say, through the flesh which the Lord had borrowed from us."* Is it not the same [light] which shone on Tabor with such intensity that, obedient to His will, it allowed even the eyes of the body to perceive it, since it was visible in the hearts of all who were purified? Like a sun, it shone from the adored Body, filling them with terror, and enveloping their hearts with light.

"May we too find ourselves with them, contemplating the glory of the Lord with unveiled faces, as if in a mirror." It would be well that we who believe these words were united in the wish expressed here by this great Doctor [of the church].

3.44

But at the Transfiguration, after it had approached us and appeared to us in the flesh, that great Light was contemplated by the pure. But today, how does anyone see it, and how is it possible to conceive it? If you wish to know, go and learn from those who see, as I too have learned from them. As David said: *"I believed. That is why I have spoken"*[182] We should add what the Apostle said: *"We too believe, this is why we speak."*[183]

He who has detached himself from material posessions, from human glory, and from carnal pleasure, in order to embrace life according to the Gospel; someone who is confirmed in this renunciation, submitting to those who have reached adulthood formed according to Christ;[184] sees the dispassionate, sacred and divine love flare up very strongly within him. He desires God above all nature, and [seeks] a union with Him that transcends the very cosmos. Entirely possessed by that desire,[185] he finds it necessary to carefully observe the activities of the body[186] and the powers of the psyche, in the hope that he might find in them a way to unite himself to God.[187] He then learns, either by himself or from experienced men, that some of these are altogether irrational, while there are other actions which, even when they contain an element of reason, cannot defend themselves well against sensations.

As to opinions and thoughts, although they arise from the reasoning power, they are not free from memories of sensations, which is to say, from the imagination. On the other hand, he has the wisdom to understand that the psychic mind is the organ by which they attain their ends. For the Apostle also said: *"The man of the psyche does not receive the things of the Spirit."*[188]

As he searches for a life that goes beyond everything, which is truly noetic and not mixed with things from here below, he listens to the words of Nilus, so wise in things divine: *"Even when the nous rises above corporeal contemplation, it does not yet have a perfect view of the place of God. For it can only know concepts, and shares in their multiplicity."*[189] And again: *"And even when the nous is simply conceptualising, it is very far from God."*[190]

3.45

But we learn, from the great Dionysius, as well as the celebrated Maximos, that our nous possesses on the one hand a power that is able to see conceptual[191] things, and on the other hand a power of union. This transcends the nature of the nous, and allows it to attach itself to what is beyond it,[192] seeking for a higher faculty that we possess, a unique, perfect, unified being that is absolutely inseparable from us. It is this which delimits and unifies the analyses of reason on which scientific certainty is founded, and which progresses by contracting and dividing, rather like creeping animals. This faculty is therefore the form of all forms.[193]

If, in fact, the nous descends into these forms, and, through them, into the multiplicity of life, communicating its activities into every faculty, it yet has a different activity that is higher than this. It may serve itself by itself, but it can also subsist by itself when it separates from the present instability of life, ever-changing and earthbound. This is like a knight[194] who possesses an activity different and higher than that which he uses for driving; so that not only when he is on

137

the ground, but also when he is on horseback or in his chariot, he can carry out this action within himself, on condition that he does not entirely abandon himself to the attention needed for driving.

And the nous, too, if it is not wholly and at all times turned towards the [world] below, can enjoy a higher and sublime activity. It is true that this is much more difficult than for the knight, for by nature it is linked to the body, entangled in knowledge of physical forms, and in all that comes from life here below, diverse and difficult to separate from. Therefore, when the nous gives itself to its own activity, which consists in turning and watching itself, then, when it transcends itself through this, it can be united to God.

3.46

This is why someone who wishes passionately to live with God flees the life that is subject to judgement. He chooses the monastic life, and is a stranger to marriage. He wishes to live without trouble or care in the sanctuary of Hesychia, far from all intercourse with the outside world. He frees his psyche, as far as is possible, from every material link, and attaches his nous to unceasing prayer to God. By this, he concentrates himself entirely within and finds a new and indescribable way of ascending to heaven through what we might call the elusive darkness of interior silence.

With indescribable joy, he carefully attaches his nous there in a silence which is absolutely simple, complete, and full of sweetness, flying beyond all creatures. Going right out from himself like this, and giving himself completely to God, he sees the glory of God, and contemplates the divine light, which is not simply sensible but forms the well loved and holy vision enjoyed by psyches and nouses without stain.

When using its noetic sense in union with what is beyond it, no nous can see without this light, just as no bodily eye can see without the light of the senses.

In this way, our nous goes out of itself and unites with God, at the same time transcending itself. God, on His part, also goes out of Himself, and unites with our nous in this way, in an action of condescending grace.[195] *"In the excess of His goodness, He, who is above everything and transcends all things, goes out of Himself without dividing Himself, as if enchanted by desire and love."*[196] In this very union, which transcends the nous, He unites Himself to us. Moreover, it is not only with us that God unites by condescending grace, but also with the heavenly angels. Again we learned this from Saint Macarius: *"In His infinite kindness,"* he says, *"the Great-One-beyond-being made himself small so that he could mingle with His noetic creatures, I mean with the psyches of the saints, and with the angels, so that through His divinity they too can participate in the immortal life."*[197]

How could He not go as far as this in His condescension, He who humbled Himself as far as the flesh, as far as the flesh of death,[198] as far as death on the cross,[199] in order to lift the veil of darkness drawn over the psyche after the fall, and so communicate his light, as the same saint taught us in the chapter mentioned at the beginning?

Tremble, then, you men without faith who lead others into faithlessness; you blind who wish to lead the blind;[200] you who move so very far from God, dragging others with you; you who teach that God is not light, because you yourselves do not see [the light]. Tremble, you who not only turn your own eyes away from the light to return to darkness, but call the light 'darkness,' making the great condescension of God become vain by this, [at least] as far as you are concerned!

You would not be in this 'pathetic state' if you had believed the words of the fathers, for those who believe give evidence of a great reverence, not only for the supernatural grace, but also for graces that are controversial. *"There exists,"* says Saint Mark, *"a grace which the infant does not know, but which one should neither anath-ematise, since it may be true, nor accept, as it may lead to delu-sion.* "There exists, you see, a grace that is true, but which is different from dogmatic truth; For what is controversial in dogmatic truth? So there is an active and manifest grace which is beyond knowledge. Because of this, it is not good to assume that grace which has not yet been put to the test is therefore illusion. This is why the divine Nilus also counsels us to ask God to clarify phenomena of this kind: *"At that moment,"* he said, *"pray with fervour for God Himself to enlighten you, as soon as possible, on whether a vision comes from Him, and that, if it does not come from Him, He will drive the delusion far from you."*

Certainly, the fathers have never hesitated to explain to us what are the signs of delusion, and what of truth. *"A delusion, in fact, even if it imitates the face of goodness, even if it clothes itself in colourful appearances, will not cause a good action. It will not lead us to hate the world, nor to despise the glory of men, nor to desire heavenly things, nor to repress harmful thoughts. It will not obtain for us spiritual rest, joy, peace or humility. It will not bring pleasures and passions to an end, nor put the psyche in good dispositions. All these virtues are produced by grace, while delusions have the opposite result."*

Some people who have much experience will already have defined the particular characteristics of noetic vision. These can be proved by the effects it produces. *"By these effects,"* it is said, *"you will know if the noetic light that shone in your psyche comes from God or Satan; So you will not consider He who has destroyed the illusion as a deceiver, nor will you take illusion for truth."*[201]

3.49

In the present age, even the light that is free from illusion does not give us infallibility: *"He who says that it does,"* says one of the fathers, *"is in the party of the wolves."* How far they wander from the truth, those who use the excuse of human weaknesses to say that men who have received grace are mistaken. They do not hear the author of *The Ladder*, who says to us: *"No human being, but only an angel, can avoid the mistakes that come from sins."* [202] And again: *"Certain people discover their humility through their weaknesses, and thanks to their faults they are reconciled to the Mother of grace."* As men, it is not angelic dispassion which we seek, but human dispassion. According to the same saint,: *"you will know unmistakably that it is within you when you feel an inexpressible abundance of light, and an inexpressible desire*[203] *for prayer."*

Again: *"Only the psyche which is liberated from every bad predisposition can contemplate the divine light. But many people possess a knowledge of the divine doctrines while they still have predispositions."*

And again: *"Those who have weak psyches recognise the watch that the Lord keeps over them by other signs, while the perfect recognise it by the presence of the Spirit."*

And again: *"Among those who are at the elementary stage, the addition of humility gives certainty that they are progressing according to God's will.*

"In those who are midway, it is their retreat before combat.

"Among the perfect, the increase and great abundance of divine light." [204]

3.50

Therefore, if this noetic light not only gives knowledge, as the fathers said, but is itself knowledge, then if a great abundance of this light is proof of perfection which is pleasing to God, the life of Solomon would be more perfect and more pleasing to God than those of all the saints since the beginning of the ages, to say nothing of the Greeks we admire for the abundance of their wisdom! Yet this light sometimes illumines certain novices, although less distinctly. It also leads to increased humility in the perfect, although this appears different from with the novices. The same father adds: *"To the perfect, the smallest things are never trivial, while to small people, even great things are never quite perfect."*

141

And so that you will know clearly that in His love towards men, divine grace also shines on these little ones, listen to the admirable Diadochos: *"At the beginning,"* he says, *"we usually feel very strongly that the psyche is illumined by its own light through grace. In the middle of the contest, grace generally acts within the psyche, for the most part without our recognising it.'"* [205]

According to Nilus, who spoke in the Spirit: *"The Holy Spirit, sympathising with our weakness, comes to visit us even when we are impure. As long as He finds our nous praying with the desire for true prayer, He enters there and scatters all the phalanx of thoughts and conceptions that besiege it."* [206]

And Saint Macarius said: *"God is good: in His Love for men, He satisfies the petitions of those who pray to Him. The divine grace sometimes comes to dwell in those who exhaust themselves in prayer, even if they have not manifested equal zeal towards the other virtues. Prayer is given to such a person in proportion to grace, in joy according to what he had asked from God, although he remains deprived of all the other good things. It is not necessary, however, that he disregards these other good things, but that, by perseverance and practice in this struggle, he strives in his heart to become obliging and obedient to God, seeking to acquire all the virtues. Thus, indeed, the grace of prayer granted by the Spirit will go on to bear fruit, bringing with it true humility, a real love, and all the array of virtues that he had asked for from the beginning of his struggle."* [207]

3.51

Do you see the importance of calling on the Father? He rebuilds what remains to be built, but does not expose the foundations on the pretext that the walls are not yet rebuilt. Nor does He knock these down because the roof has not been put on. He knows, in fact, he understands by experience, that the kingdom of heaven is sown like a grain of mustard in us. It is the smallest of all seeds, but then it becomes so big, and so far surpasses all the powers of the psyche, that it becomes a pleasant nesting place for the birds of the sky. [208]

But these people of whom you speak judge because they lack judgement. In their inexperience, they find themselves lacking in what could have been useful to their brothers. Impudently taking to themselves the judgement which belongs to God, they say that one person rather than another is worthy of grace, choosing any basis they like for this judgement. But it is for God alone to designate those who are worthy of His own grace.

If He himself has welcomed a man, says the Apostle, *"who are you, to judge the servant of another?"*[209] As for us, let us then go back to the point where we began, and, adding a few more words, end this treatise, which is beginning to become very long.

3.52

Someone who does not believe in the great mystery of New Grace, who is blind to the hope of deification, cannot disdain the pleasures of flesh, money, riches, or human glory. If he does so for a brief moment, it is immediately superseded by pride at having attained perfection, so that he falls back into the category of the impure. Someone who desires this hope, even someone who has accomplished all the good actions, seeks for perfection that is the more than perfect and even infinite. He does not think about what he has [already] acquired, and so he progresses in humility. He thinks sometimes of the superiority of the saints who preceded him, sometimes of the *great abundance* of the divine love towards men. In sorrow he weeps and cries out, like Isaiah: *"Woe to me! I am impure, I have unclean lips, for my eyes have seen the Lord Sabaoth."*[210] But this sorrow brings progress in purification, and the Lord of grace adds consolation and illumination.

This is why John Climacus, who teaches from experience, says to us: *"The depth of sorrow has seen consolation, and purity of heart has received illumination."*[211] So it is the purified heart which receives this illumination, although even an impure heart can take in what one can say or know on the subject of God.

It is therefore evident that this illumination surpasses all words and all knowledge, whether we call it *'knowledge,'* or 'noesis,' because it is the Spirit which provided it to the nous. *"It acts,"* it is said, *"through another form of noesis, a spiritual form which is withheld even from faithful hearts, unless they have been purified by works."* This is why He who produced the vision and why he is Himself its object, God, the light of the pure heart, says: *"Blessed are the pure in heart, for they shall see God."* [212] How would they be blessed, if this vision was knowledge of a kind which the impure might possess? The one who was illumined and who gave a definition of illumination has therefore spoken well. Illumination is not a [kind of] knowledge, but an *"indescribable activity,*[213] *which we see without seeing,"* since the vision is not through the senses, and *"which we recognise without knowing,"*[214] since it is not by means of thought.

I could add other testimonies, but I fear even these have been offered in vain. For, according to the same saint, *"he who wants to tell in words about the perception and action of divine illumination to those who have not tasted it, is like somebody who wishes to use words to describe the taste of honey to those who have never tasted it."*

It is to you, however, that our words are addressed, so that you may know with certainty what is true, and so that you will know that we too agree with the words of the fathers.

NOTES

NOTES TO INTRODUCTION

1. 1 Corinthians 9:24-27.
2. Meyendorff - *A Study of Gregory Palamas,* 134. SVS. Crestwood, New York, 1998.
3 Nicholas Gendle, *Gregory Palamas - The Triads* - Paulist Press, New York and SPCK, London. 1983.
4: Dionysius the Areopagite - *The Ecclesiastical hierarchy.* Quoted in Meyendorff - *A Study of Gregory Palamas,* SVS. Crestwood, New York, 1998
5. Meyedorff - *A Study of Gregory Palamas,* 116. SVS. Crestwood, New York, 1998
6. Triads Vol.1. Part 3: 15
7. Meyendorff - *A Study of Gregory Palamas,* 134. SVS. Crestwood, New York, 1998

NOTES TO PART I

1. Gr: *agnoia,* which - for Evagrius and others of the spiritual tradition - is the opposite of *gnosis,* and is said to represent a state of spiritual and noetic emptiness which can be filled only by grace. (See Triad 1:3.3)
2. Gr: *paedeia* – The Periclean Greek word for education, which originally referred to an education that included philosophy, aesthetics and physical exercises, but in this context describes it as referring to a Hellenic form of education of Palamas' time. In the approach of those who supported this, the intellectual and speculative elements of classical Greek thought that had been eliminated by the fathers of the church were then being reintroduced.
3. Barlaam: *Letter 3 to Palamas.*
4. Gr: *gnosis* - knowledge
5. According to the fathers, noetic knowledge was of the nous, and nous was the highest power of psyche: the 'eye of the psyche.' But it appears that the intellectuals of the period we are studying regarded the nous as intellect in the modern sense, discursive and logical, whereas the nous of the fathers of the church was something different from this.
6. Gr: *Psyche* - means life or vitality, soul, and mind.
7. These methods are taken from Barlaam: *Letter 1 to Palamas. Epistle II ad eodem.*
8. 1 Peter 3:15.
9. Hebrews 13:9 *"Be not carried about with divers and strange doctrines. For it is a good thing that the heart be established with grace; not with meats, which have not profited them that have been occupied therein."*
10. This idea that the hesychast tradition is founded in experience is important in the teaching represented by Palamas.

11. A proverb of the times, which appears to have been a favourite with Palamas.

12. Gr: *hoi sophoi.* Those wise ones. Palamas phrase for the intellectuals.

13. Meyendorff, in his French translation, notes that according to Barlaam the main value of the Greek philosophers was to affirm the unknowability of God and so define the limits of human knowledge.

14. Gr. *demiurgiko no*: Divine Creative Nous.

15. Romans 11:34.

16. 'Gr: *logois,* reasons in the sense of reasons why - causes or purposes.

17. cf. 1 Corinthians 1:17-25.

18. 1 Corinthians 8:1.

19. Gr: *nous sarkos.* Cf. Colossians 2:18.

20. 1. Corinthians 1:26.

21. According to some sources, if we become aware of these images of logoi within our hearts and learn to live by them, this will lead us toward salvation. Sin is what obscures them and prevents their playing their proper part in our lives.

22. Gr. *Alethous theorias* - seems to refer to contemplative truth.

23. Gr. sundiaioniseis = "together through the ages" sun + dia + aion; root is aion, *"an age, or eternity"*

24. Romans 16:27. *"To God only wise, be glory through Jesus Christ for ever. Amen."*

25. The phenomena of overoxygenation have no spiritual significance.

26. Gr: *mellontos aionos*: The age to come. According to certain of the early fathers, the age to come can be found at some far future time after death, but it can also be reached by sufficiently purified individuals in this life. That is to say, it is a state, not a place.

27. Palamas links the idea of becoming perfect (cf. Matthew 5:48.) with 1 Corinthians 14:20 *"Brethren, be not children in understanding: howbeit in malice be ye children, but in understanding be men."*

28. Philippians 3:15 *"Let us therefore, as many as be perfect, be like-minded: and if in any thing ye be otherwise minded, God shall reveal even this unto you."*

29. 1 Corinthians 2:6.

30. Dionysius the Areopagite; *Ecclesiastical Hierarchy* II.

31. John the Baptist.

32. Matthew 11:11. *"Verily I say unto you, Among them that are born of women there hath not risen a greater than John the Baptist: notwithstanding he that is least in the kingdom of heaven is greater than he."*

33. Cf. John 8:58

34. John 18:37.

35. Christ as the image or icon of God in humanity.

36. As Barlaam and the intellectuals had said.

37. Matthew 19:21.

38. Cf. Matthew 16:24; Mark 8:34; Luke 9:23.

39. 1 Corinthians 1:27.

40. 1 Corinthians 1:20.

41. Christ as the image or icon of God in humanity. 1 Corinthians 1:21.

42. Ibid.

43. I Corinthians 1:30 – but perhaps not quite as we know that sentence, given in the King James version as: *"But of him are ye in Christ Jesus, who of God is made unto us wisdom, and righteousness, and sanctification, and redemption:"*

44. John 1:9.

45. 2 Peter 1:19.

46. A wick, perhaps an image of a way of feeding a clear and steady light in the psyche?

47. Meyendorff points out that St. John Climacus recommends the opposite to this; not to allow ourselves to grow old in our studies. *Ladder XXVI.*

48. The nous was often described by the early fathers as the *eye of the psyche.*

49. Meyendorff reports that Palamas attitude towards profane studies agrees exactly with the official decisions of the Byzantine church, and with the condemnation, made in 1082, *against those who practice the Hellenic sciences, not only in private and in education, but in holding their own opinions.* But the reason for this statement is obviously that to practice these sciences is seen as a serious obstacle to salvation.

50. Saint Gregory Nazianzen.

51. Gr: *iuggas* - charm, passionate yearning.

52. Proverbs 1:7.

53. Compunction: Gr: *katanuxei*, lit. pricking (of the heart).

54. Deuteronomy 6:5. *"And thou shalt love the Lord they God with all thine heart, and with all thine psyche, and with all thy might."*

55. Meyendorff links this image to Evagrius, Macarius, and Maximos and the images of purification to Gregory of Nyssa.

56. Exodus 5:17.

57. Acts 17:21.

58. In St. Basil s *Homily on Psalm XLV.* We can see here that it is easy and probably correct to assume from this that the term wicked spirits refers to the corrupted spirits of the individuals who act in this way, not to creatures of the air, in any superstitious sense.

59. Proverbs 1:2.

60. In St. Basil s Homily XII on Proverbs 1:6.

61. Romans 1:22.

62. 1 Corinthians 2:6.

63. Basil s *Epistle 223.*

64. Matthew 16:3. But the Greek does not translate exactly. For Palamas, the Kingdom is not a place, but the coming of divine authority into our lives.

65. James 1:5. *"If any of you lack wisdom, let him ask of God, that giveth to all men liberally, and upbraideth not; and it shall be given him."*

66. Romans 2:13.

67. Luke 12:47-48.

68. St. John Chrysostom. *Homily IV:4.*

69. Cf. 1 Corinthians 1:17. *"For Christ sent me not to baptise, but to preach the gospel: not with wisdom of words, lest the cross of Christ should be made of none effect."*

70. Cf. 1 Corinthians 2:4. *"And my speech and my preaching was not with enticing words of man s wisdom, but in demonstration of the Spirit and of power."*

71. 1 Corinthians 2:2. *"For I determined not to know any thing among you, save Jesus Christ, and him crucified."*

72. 1 Corinthians 8:1.

73. Ephesians 4:22. Colossians 3:9.

74. James 3:17.

75. 1 Corinthians 1:21, 24 etc.

76. James 3:15.

77. 1 Corinthians 2:14. *"But the natural man receiveth not the things of the Spirit of God: for they are foolishness unto him: neither can he know them, because they are spiritually discerned."*

78. For this important theme of the two kinds of knowledge, see Saint Maximus, *Centuries on Gnosis, 1.22.*

79. Deuteronomy 15:9 – a formula adopted by all Christian spirituals in preference to *'gnose sueton',*

80. *Gnose sueton'* – a key element in this part of the book, which strives to distinguish clearly between the attentiveness of the spirituals and the 'know yourself' of the philosophers.

81. Acts 16:17

82. 2 Corinthians 11:14.

83. 2 Corinthians 11:15.

84. Numenius of Apame.

85. 1 Corinthians 2:16.

86. Isaiah 55:9. 87. James 1:17.

87. James 1:17.

88. Jeremiah 10:11.

89. John 1:9.

90. A summary of the image and terms in Barlaam's *Second Letter.*

91. Samuel 17:36.

92. 1 Corinthians 1:20.

93. Dionysius the Areopagite, *The Divine Names. IV.19.*

94. The concept of angels as second lights - perhaps reflected lights - is found particularly in Gregory Nazianzus.

95. John 1:9.

96. Romans 3:31.

97. John 5:39.

98. John 5:46.

99. The Greek has unspeakable, which is to be taken literally.

100. Cf. 1 Corinthians 2:14.

101. Cf. Romans 1:25.

102. 1 Corinthians 1:21

103. Romans 1:21. *"Because, when they knew God, they glorified him not as God, neither were thankful; but became vain in their imaginations, and their foolish heart was darkened."*

104. Romans 1:28. *"And even as they did not like to retain God in their knowledge God gave them over to a reprobate mind, to do those things which are not convenient;"*

105. Romans 1:25.

106. 1 Corinthians 1:25.

107. Plato. *Phaedrus. 245a.*

108. Plato. Timaeus. *27cd.*

109. This conclusion is attributed to Porphyry.

110. Homer. *The Iliad. I.5.1.*

111. This phrase, *in his psyche,* makes the meaning of the whole passage clear.

112. Wisdom 1:5.

113. 1 Corinthians 10:21. *"Ye cannot drink the cup of the Lord, and the cup of devils: ye cannot be partakers of the Lord s table, and of the table of devils."*

114. 1 Corinthians 1:21. *"For after that in the wisdom of God the world by wisdom knew not God, it pleased God by the foolishness of preaching to save them that believe."*

115. Pseudo-Dionysius: *Letters.VII.*

116. Pseudo-Dionysius: *The Divine Names. IV.23.*

117. Pseudo-Dionysius: *Letters.VII.*

118. 1 Corinthians 1:21.

119. 1 Corinthians 2:7. *"But we speak the wisdom of God in a mystery, even the hidden wisdom, which God ordained before the world unto our glory:"*

120. 1 Corinthians 2:6.

121. 1 Corinthians 2:8.

122. 1 Corinthians 1.30.

123. Romans 1.21.

124. Refers to the doctrine of the World Soul in Plato's *Timaeus.*

125. Matthew 7:18.

126. Cf. Gregory of Nyssa - *On the Making of Man* - against the doctrine of the transmigration of souls.

127. 1 Corinthians 2:4. *"Where is the wise? where is the scribe? where is the disputant of this world? hath not God made foolish the wisdom of this world?"*

128.1 Corinthians 2:13.

129. 1 Corinthians 1:26.

130. Romans 1:22.

131. 1 Corinthians 1:20.

132. Colossians 2:8.

133. 1 Corinthians 2:6.

134. Cf. Dionysius the Areopagite, *on the Divine Names, 7:2.*

135. Gr: *anoun* - without nous or without understanding.

136. James 3:15.

151

137. This image was used by Barlaam in his second letter.

138. Meyendorff says that this is a reference to Genesis 4:7, in the Septuagint version, which says: *"If you make your offering correctly without dividing correctly, do you not sin?*

139. St.Isaac of Nineveh (Isaac the Syrian.) *Homily 72.*

140. 1 Corinthians 2:9.

141. But how can one remove the 'extremities' of an idea while keeping the meaning? This depends on a subtle understanding of the ancient idea of antinomies that provides a method of distinguishing the worldly from the divine.

142. 2 Corinthians 1:12.

143. 1 Corinthians 1:26.

144. Cf. 1 Timothy 3:7.

145. Gregory the Theologian, *Sermon 41:14.* Palamas also quotes these passages in the Second Triad, Pt.1 Sect.12.

146. Cf. Acts 13:9.

147. 2 Corinthians 12:2-4.

148. 1 Corinthians 1:6.

149. 1 Corinthians 2:6.

150. 1 Corinthians 1:18.

151. John 10:5.

152. St. Gregory of Nyssa - *Epistle 8.*

153. Basil the Great, *Commentary on Psalm 14.*

154. Dionysius the Areopagite, *Ecclesiastical Hierarchy, 2.*

155. St. John Chrysostom. *Homily 1 on Matthew; 4-5.*

156. St.Gregory Nazianzus, *Homily 16, 2.*

157. St. Cyril. *Commentary on the Psalms.*

158. Ecclesiastes 1:18.

159. This text is actually not by Gregory of Nyssa, but Gregory of Agrigente.

1. Song of Songs 5:2.
2. Psalm 139 11.
3. Luke 10:16.
4. Barlaam says in his Fifth Letter that the nous enters and leaves through the nostrils in time with the breathing.
5. I Corinthians 6:19.
6. Cf. Hebrews 3:6.
7. 2 Corinthians 6:16.
8. Meyendorff reports this as a Manichean survival in the Messalian heresy, after Barlaam had earlier accused the hesychasts of being heretics like the Messalians and Euchites.
9. Meyendorff also comments that many teachers of Christian spirituality say that the body is not evil in itself.
10. Psalm 62 (63) 1.
11. Psalm 83 (84) 12.
12. Cf. Isaiah 16:18.
13. Isaiah 26:18. This should be taken almost literally.
14. Romans 7:24.
15. Romans 7:14.
16. Romans 7:18.
17. Romans 7:23.
18. Romans 8:2. *"But I see another law in my members, warring against the law of my nous, and bringing me into captivity to the law of sin which is in my members."*
19. Gr: *episkopen* = lit. oversight, this word is related to the word for Bishop.
20. Gr: *somatos;* not Paul's flesh or sarx, but the physical body itself.
21. Gr: *Egkrateia.* Self-control or temperance.
22. Gr: *Agape.* unselfish love.
23. Gr. *Nepsin.* Watchfulness or sobriety.
24. 2 Corinthians 4:6.
25. 2 Corinthians 4:7.
26. Gr: Pnevmatikos.
27. Cf. Gregory of Nyssa.
28. See reference to Pseudo-Macarius a few lines below.
29. Matthew 15:11.
30. Matthew 15:19.
31. Cf: Macarius - *Homily, 15:20.*
32. The heart is the seat of thought, and attention is an action of the nous. So to bring attention to thought, we bring the nous into the inmost heart.
33. Macarius - *Homily, 15.* In this sermon, one phrase recalls what has just been said.

34. Gr: Hesychia.

35. Meyendorff says that the application of this text from Psalm 44(45) to the spiritual life probably goes back to Origen.

36. Galatians 4:6.

37. Luke 17:21.

38. Proverbs 27:21.

39. Proverbs 2:5.

40. St. John Climacus, Ladder, 26.   41. 2 Corinthians 1:22.

42. Remember that the daemons referred to by Palamas are the lesser gods or minor causes referred to by the Platonists. The early Greek church saw these daemons as a wrong explanation given by those who did not know God.

43. 1 Timothy 6:20. *"O Timothy, keep that which is committed to thy trust, avoiding profane and vain babblings, and oppositions of science falsely so called:"*

44. Basil the Great, *Homily XII on Proverbs 7.*

45. 1 Corinthians 2:14-15. But the natural man receiveth not the things of the Spirit of God: for they are foolishness unto him: neither can he know them, because they are spiritually discerned.

46. Dionysius the Areopagite; *The Divine Names. 4:9.*

47. Ibid.

48. St.Basil. *Epistle 2, to St.Gregory Naziansus.* This concept of the faultless action that draws the pure nous to God is also found in Indian philosophy in the idea of the Method of Cause and Effect.

49. Dionysius the Areopagite; *The Divine Names. 4:9.*

50. See Barlaam s *Letter to Ignatius.*

51. St.John Climacus - *Ladder. 27.*

52. For Meyendorff, this is union with Christ. For the translators of the Philokalia into English, it is the union of the nous with the matter of the body. As Palamas says later, the matter of the body finds its life in Christ.

53. It sometimes seems from usage that this originally implied not just a person who lives alone but a unified, self-sufficient individual.

54. In the Method of Symeon the New Theologian.

55. Cf. Dionysius the Areopagite; *The Divine Names. 4:9.*

56. I Corinthians 13:7.

57. The Fall as a transgression against God s commandment.

58. Cf: Macarius - *Homilies, 16:7.* Climacus - *Ladder 25.*

59. Cf. Dionysius the Areopagite; *The Divine Names. 4:8.*

60. Cf. Symeon the New Theologian. *Three methods of Attention and Prayer.* Palamas used the same description in his second letter to Barlaam.

61. Gr: *Noeton theros.*

62. This is the position in which Japanese thought discovers the force known as hara.

63. Cf. Romans 7:23.

64. Titus 3:5. *"Not by works of righteousness which we have done, but according to his mercy he saved us, by the washing of regeneration, and renewing of the Holy Ghost;"* In this text, this refers to baptism.

65. Luke 11:26.

66. Deuteronomy 15:9.

67. Ibid.

68. Ecclesiastes 10:4.

69. Psalm 7:10.

70. 1 Corinthians 11 31.

71 Psalm 138 (139) 11.

72. A commentary on Genesis 6:1-6.

73. Romans 8:11 *"But if the Spirit of him that raised up Jesus from the dead dwell in you, he that raised up Christ from the dead shall also quicken your mortal bodies by his Spirit that dwelleth in you."*

74. Passage from I Kings 18 as taken from Palamas *Second letter to Barlaam.*

75. Cf: Matthew 23:25, and Luke 11:39.

76. Luke 18:13 And the publican, standing afar off, would not lift up so much as his eyes unto heaven, but smote upon his breast, saying, God be merciful to me a sinner.

77. As if they thought their brains were in their navels.

78. Barlaam advised his associate Ignatius to abandon the sobriety of the hesychasts and find another method.

79. People who consider that their psyche is in their stomach.

80. Psalm 40:8.

81. Cf. Isaiah 16:11.

82. Barlaam himself referred to the unknowability of God and never pretended to see anything more than shadows and images.

83. Meyendorff says that the *Guarding of the Heart*, by Nicephorus, is actually an anthology of patristic texts and lives of saints, with a brief announcement about the psychophysical method.

84. Symeon and Nicephorus.

85. A play on the meaning of his name, Theoleptus.

86. Philotheus, in his *Ecomion*, reports that Palamas was himself initiated into the hesychastic life by Theoleptus of Philadelphia.

87. Psalm 103:1

1. Variation on Colossians 2:18.
2. Gr: *gnosis.*
3. Delusion as a state, not an item of misinformation - Gr: planes, wandering: Used to described the state of the nous when it wanders, when it is unstable because disturbed by the activities of the psyche.
4. On 10th October in the year 351, at Nike in Thrace, the Arians obtained from a delegation of Orthodox bishops, members of the council of Rimini, the signing of a formula which disowned the decisions of Nicea, the most important of the seven Ecumenical Councils of the early church which, in AD 325, defined the faith of the early church.
5. Gr: *monologisto proseuche.*
6. Gr: *dianoian.*
7. Gr: *archen,* cause, beginning, fundamental principle; a key word that was developed progressively in classical Greek philosophy, and fills a key position in Genesis and in the first verse of St. John s Gospel: *"In the beginning (archen) was the Word."*
8. Gr: *logickes psyches.*
9. This refers to Peter 2:4, which says that: *"! God spared not the angels that sinned, but cast them down to hell, and delivered them into chains of darkness."*
10. 2 Corinthians 4:6
11. Gr: *noeton*
12. Gr: *noeron.*
13. When the light visibly radiates from the body of an individual, it is said that this is evidence of the resurrection of the body. If we understand Palamas teaching we will understand this statement.
14. Gr: *gnosis*
15 Dionysius the Areopagite - *The Divine Names - in Pseudo-Dionysius. the Complete Works* - New York, 1987 Paulist Press P75 para.4.
16 Gr: *hieroi andres.*
17. John 17:22 *"And the glory which thou gavest me I have given them; that they may be one, even as we are one:"*
18. The light revealed to the eyes of the disciples when our Lord was transfigured on the mountain. Cf: Matthew 17:1-3, Mark 9:2-13, Luke 9:28-36.
19. St.Andrew of Crete, *Homily VII.*
20. A pseudonym for Evagrius of Pontus.
21. Exodus 24:2.
22 The relevant text is quoted in Evagrius *Kephalia Gnostica.*
23. 2 Corinthians 4:6.
24. Macarius - Homily 5:10.
25. Diadochus - *On Spiritual Knowledge and Discrimination.*

26. Maximos. *Gnostic Centuries* I. 31.

27. Saint Basil the Great says that human knowledge is gained by efforts of study and practice, while the knowledge given by God depends on His justice and His mercy.

28. Here Nilus is a pseudonym for Evagrius. *Practicos* 1.93.29.

29. Corinthians 4:6.

30. Psalm 12: 3.

31. Psalm 42:3.

32. Psalm 4:6.

33. CF Macarius - *The Free Mind* - 22.

34. Palamas, in the chapters that follow, reports this illumination as a real experience of an inner light, and specifically says that it is not merely figurative or symbolic.

35. In our times, this figurative use of the word light has become commonplace so that the original meaning of an inner light is almost lost.

36. Gr: *logou dynamin*

37. Gr: *theoreton* - contemplated, referring to non-sensory awareness.

38. St. Isaac the Syrian and many others have used term like this which describe the nous as the eye of the soul.

39. Gr: *noeran echon aisthesin horoe.*

40. John 14:21.

41. I Corinthians 13:12.

42. Malachi 4:2.

43. Gr: *hyperanidrumenon.*

44. The mystical knowledge which is the result of God s condescension , according to St. John Chrysostom. *Ad Theod.lapsum.* I:1.

45. Gregory the Theologian. *Homily 21:2.*

46. Matthew 25:41.

47. Cf. Philippians 2:11.

48. Perhaps in the modern sense of in the now.

49. Gr: *pneumatikon.*

50. Gr: *teleiotetos.*

51. Gr: *phroneseos.*

52 Corinthians 3:11. *"For if that which is done away was glorious, much more that which remaineth is glorious."*

53. Gr: *to athanato tou eso anthropou prosopo.*

54. 2 Corinthians 3:18 *"But we all, with open face beholding as in a glass the glory of the Lord, are changed into the same image from glory to glory, even as by the Spirit of the Lord."*

55. Gr: *epistrepse.*

56. 1 Corinthians 2:15-16. *"But he that is spiritual judgeth all things, yet he himself is judged of no man."*

57. 1 Corinthians 2:14.

58. Cf. Romans 1:22. 1 Corinthians 1:20.

59. 1 Corinthians 2:10.
60. 1 Corinthians 2:13-16. Normally translated as the mind of Christ.
61. 1 Corinthians 2:12.
62. Habakkuk 2:15.
63. 1 Corinthians 2:15.
64. Ibid.
65 Lit. But what about life.
66. Gr: *metanoias*
67. Cf. St. Basil the Great - *On Psalm 14.*
68. John 1:18.
69. Matthew 5:8
70. John 14:23.
71. Gr: *logikes eikonos.*
72. 1 Corinthians 2:10. *"But God hath revealed them unto us by his Spirit: for the Spirit searcheth all things, yea, the deep things of God."*
73. St. Basil's *2nd letter* to Gregory of Nazianzus.
74. Corinthians 2:11.
75. 1 Corinthians 2:9.
76. 1 Corinthians 2:16 *"For who hath known the mind of the Lord, that he may instruct him? But we have the mind of Christ."*
77. Gr: *noousi.*
78. Gr: *igoumeni*, same root as igumenos, the term used for an Abbot.
79. Song 1:15.
80. This connection of the dove with the betrothed goes back to Origen.
81. 1 Corinthians 6:17 *"But he that is joined unto the Lord is one spirit."*
82. Cf. Gregory of Nyssa - in *Song of Man. IV & VII.*
83. Transcendence is not caused by activity but by a cessation of the activity of the nous. Theoria (contemplation) is not just loss, but gains the extraordinary when it loses the ordinary in the meeting of passionlessness and the nous in apatheia and divine grace.
84. Gr: *Apharaisin* - abstraction, in this context, inner separation of the nous from activities in the psyche. Palamas Aristotelian background shows here. The alternative rendering of stripping-away is neo-Platonist and not Christian in implication.
85. St. Isaac s statement is relevant because traditional Christian doctrine is that admission to the divine presence is by the grace of God, not the choice of man.
86. In the computer sense of writing data & hence of storing information in memory.
87. Gr: *gnoseos*
88. Gr: *phantasia.*
89. Gr: *dianoia.*
90. Gr: *doxa.*
91. Gr: *logos.*
92. Dionysius the Areopagite - *Epistle I* Cf. *The Mystical Theology, III*
93. Gr: *gnophos* - perhaps a play on words with gnosis and pho - knowledge and light.

94. Cf. Matthew 7:6.
95. Cf. Dionysius the Areopagite - *The Mystical Theology - III.*
96. Ibid. C.
97. Gr: *apopleroseos*, related to pleroma .
98. The uncreated light.
99. *Aesthesis theia* is a term originated by Origen in *Contra Celsum* and later used by Gregory of Nyssa. Cf. J.Danielou - *Platonism et theologie mystique* - p238-239. It provides a scriptural basis for an idea which Meyendorff says is essential to Eastern Orthodox mysticism.
100. Dionysius the Areopagite - *Of the Divine Names - 7:1*
101. Dionysius the Areopagite - *Of the Divine Names - 4 : 11.*
102. Cf. 2 Corinthians 12:2.
103. Gr: *ekplexeos*; related to ekplexis; striking with a sudden shock, panic, fear, consternation. Cf. St. Isaac the Syrian - Homily 32.
104. Ibid.
105. Gr: *ekstesan*, related to our word ecstasy.
106. Cf. Macarius-Symeon, *Freedom of the Mind. 21.*
107. The phrase noetic or intelligible sun was taken by Palamas from St. Benedict.
108. Lit: en-psyched or en-souled body.
109. Mark 9:2.
110. 2 Peter 1: 16-18.
111. Gr: *aporretos*: not cannot be described, but may not be.
112. 1 Corinthians 2:13 *"Which things also we speak, not in the words which mans wisdom teacheth, but which the Holy Ghost teacheth; comparing spiritual things with spiritual."*
113. 2 Corinthians 1:12.
114. 1 Corinthians 2:13.
115. 1 Kings 19:12.
116. Isaiah 16:11. *"Wherefore my bowels shall sound like an harp for Moab, and mine inward parts for Kirharesh."*
117. 2 Kings 2:11.
118. Jeremiah 20:8-9.
119. Psalm 78:25.
120. Luke 11:13 and 18:7.
121. Cf. Dionysius the Areopagite, *The Divine names.1:5.*
122. Mark 9:2-8.
123. 2 Peter 1:16-18.
124. St. John Chrysostom.
125. Gregory Nazianzen - *Homily 40:6.*
126. Symeon Metaphrastes - *Life of St. John the Evangelist, 1*
127. Matthew 16:38 - Mark 9: 1 - Luke 9:27.
128. Gr: *photophaneias.*
129. Luke 2:8-10.

130. Macarius the Great - source uncertain.

131. 2 Peter 1:16-18.

132. Cf.Macarius-Symeon - *The Free Mind - 21.*

133. Cf. Hebrews 1:3.

134. A prayer often repeated in the Byzantine service for the dead.

135. Acts 7:55-56. Given almost exactly as in the Greek NT.

136. Acts 7:56.

137. In Greek thought, this idea of witnessing or confessing to the truth of the faith is one of proving what you witness to by sacrificing yourself for it. The implication here is that without faith you will not believe words nor even the testimony of self-sacrifice.

138. Gr: *aplanes* - without error is, literally, without wandering. The Greek word *plani* is rendered in Russian as *prelest* ; hence, a-planes: free from delusion.

139. Exodus 34:35.

140. Acts 6:15.

141. Cf. *the life of St. Mary the Egyptian.*

142. Matthew 24:30.

143. St. John Climacus.

144. Luke 22:44.

145. Psalm 118:103.

146. Psalm 63:5.

147. Matthew. 5:4.

148. Cf. Song of Songs 4:11.

149. Gr. Noeran.

150. Gr: Hyper noeran.

151. Meyendorff here suggests that this is taken from an unedited text of Macarius and so cannot be traced exactly.

152. Dionysius the Areopagite - *The Divine Names. 1:4.*

153. 1 Corinthians 15:28.

154. It can be seen externally through the senses augmented by nous, it can be seen now, in moments, again by the nous, and it can be seen in the age to come.

155. Matthew 13:43.

156. 1 Corinthians 2:9.

157. 1 Corinthians 15:44.

158. Luke 20:36.

159. Matthew 22:30. *"For in the resurrection they neither marry, nor are given in marriage, but are as the angels of God in heaven."*

160. Saint Maximos - *Gnostic Centuries - II.88.* .

161. Colossians 2:9.

162. 1 Corinthians 13:12 *"For now we see through a glass, darkly; but then face to face: now I know in part; but then shall I know even as also I am known."*

163. Psalm 90:17.

164. Revelations 2:17 *"He that hath an ear, let him hear what the Spirit saith unto the churches; To him that overcometh will I give to eat of the hidden manna, and will give him a white stone, and in the stone a new name written, which no man knoweth saving he that receiveth it."*

165. 2 Corinthians 11:14.

166. Cf. Maximos - *Scholia on The Divine Names. 13.*

167. Cf. St. Gregory Nazianzus - *Homily 40:5.*

168. Evagrius - *Practicos 1:70.*

169. From Ch. 149 in *Evagrius On Prayer,* in Climacus *ladder, 28th rung.*

170. Maximos - *Gnostic Centuries. - 2.80.*

171. Maximos - *Gnostic Centuries - 2:80.*

172. 2 Corinthians 3:3 *"Forasmuch as ye are manifestly declared to be the epistle of Christ ministered by us, written not with ink, but with the Spirit of the living God; not in tables of stone, but in fleshly tables of the heart."*

173. This same passage from Macarius is quoted in *Triad 1 Part 2,* section 3.

174. Maximos - *Centuries on Gnosis. 2:82.*

175. *Gr: aneidos* - imageless.

176. Gr: *dianoias.*

177. Dionysius the Areopagite - *The Divine Names -. 1:4.*

178. Macarius-Symeon - *Freedom of the Mind - 24.*

179. Gr: *hypostasis.*

180. Macarius-Symeon - *Freedom of the Mind - 26..*

181. Perhaps from Macarius-Symeon - *Homily 5:11.*

182. Psalm 116:10.

183. 2 Corinthians 4:13.

184. Ephesians 4:13. *"Until we all come in the unity of the faith, and of the knowledge of the Son of God, unto a perfect man, unto the measure of the stature of the fullness of Christ:"*

185. Gr: *Eroti.*

186. Gr: *tas somatikas energeias.*

187. Gr: *tas psychikas dynameis.*

188. 1 Corinthians 2:14. *"But the natural man receiveth not the things of the Spirit of God, for they are foolishness unto him; neither can he know them, because they are spiritually discerned."*

189. Evagrius of Pontus - *On Prayer - 57.*

190. Ibid - 56.

191. Gr: *Ta noeta.*

192. Dionysius the Areopagite - *The Divine Names - 7:1.*

193. Gr: eidos ousa ton eidon.

194. Possible source of the description of the personality type of the same name in Boris Mouravieff - *Gnosis,* Volume 2.

195. St. Maximos - *Gnostic Centuries. 1:31.*

196. Dionysius the Areopagite - *the Divine Names - 4:13.*

197. Macarius-Symeon - *Elevation of the Mind - 6.*

198. Cf. Romans 7:24.
199. Philippians 2:8
200. Matthew 15:14.
201 Macarius-Symeon - *On Patience - 13.*
202. Cf. St. John Climacus - *The Ladder - 4.*
203. Gr: *eroti.*
204. St. John Climacus - *The Ladder - 26.*
205. Diadochus - *Caput 69.*
206. Evagrius, under the pseudonym Nilus - *On Prayer - 62.*
207. From Macarius - *Homily 19* or Macarius-Symeon - *The Free Mind - 18-19.*
208. Matthew 13: 31-32.
209. Romans 14:4.
210. Cf. Isaiah 6:5.
211. St. John Climacus - *The Ladder - 7.*
212. Matthew 5:8.
213. Gr: *energeia* - something like the modern definition of energy as activity (kinetic energy).
214. Climacus - *Ibid.*

PRAXIS

BOOKS ON ESOTERIC CHRISTIANITY, CHRISTIAN MYSTICISM, AND RELATED SUBJECTS

Saint Theophan the Recluse

THE HEART OF SALVATION

The life and teachings of Theophan the Recluse, greatest of Russia's masters of inner Christianity, compiler of the fullest version of the Russian 'Philokalia'. The book draws on seven years of study in the ancient monasteries of the Middle East and is rooted in the richly practical spirituality of 19th Century Russia. It is of great practical significance to serious students of hesychastic spirituality.

ISBN 1-872292-02-X

208PP PB$19.95 £14.95

THE PATH OF PRAYER

St. Theophan's Four Sermons on Prayer

A full and rich introduction to the use of daily and liturgical prayer as a method of spiritual development by this researcher, bishop, hermit and staretz whose correspondence guided thousands.

ISBN 1-872292-14-3 96 PP   PB $11.95, £9.95

HARDBOUND $15.95, £11.95

TURNING WITHIN

BY THOMAS JOHNSON-MEDLAND

In this little book by an American Orthodox Deacon you will find a familiar voice speaking of 'interior prayer.' What the author has learned can help others to pray.

ISBN 1-872292-21-6, 45 PP, PB, $9.95   £7.50

TAPES FROM THE PHILOKALIA

Chosen by translator G.E.H. Palmer for a blind friend, read by Sergei Kadloubovsky from the original English translation of the 'Philokalia' published by Faber, these texts 'on watchfulness and holiness' are a meaningful and moving expression of the inner traditions of the early church fathers.

TWO 90 MIN. AUDIO TAPES : $19.95. £14.95

1000 YEARS ARE AS ONE DAY

A sensitive one-hour video documentary on the monasteries of Mount Athos, giving an in-depth view of life and liturgy in this remarkable spiritual community - made for German television, and now available in the US.

DISTRIBUTED BY PRAXIS ONLY IN USA - $50.00

by Robin Amis
A DIFFERENT CHRISTIANITY

After editing Mouravieff, Ouspensky and Theophan, Robin Amis, director of Praxis Institute, has finally written his own book, *A Different Christianity*, the distillation of more than fourteen years of research into traditional sources of the Royal Way, a Christian spiritual discipline little known to the Western world.

PAPER ISBN 0-791425-72-X $29.95   £24.50
HARDCOVER ISBN 0-791425-71-1 $59.90   £49.95

WHO WRITES THE WAVES?
40 years of poems by Robin Amis.

Often read in English poetry readings in the late sixties, these poems have an almost classical lyricism, and touch on the deepest questions of the inner life.

96 PAGES, HANDBND ISBN 1-872292-03-8 $19.95. £15.95

PRAXIS MONOGRAPHS

BY BORIS MOURAVIEFF

NO.1 THE PROBLEM OF THE NEW MAN

A clear vision of the dangers of our current course, and an outline of possibilities for an individual regeneration that could assist in avoiding such a catastrophe.

ISBN 1-872292-20-8 $5.95 £3.95

NO 2. THE SUBSTANTIAL AND THE ESSENTIAL

A further study of the problem of individual regeneration defining the task of the seeker at this crucial point in history.

ISBN 1-872292-21-6 $5.95 £3.95

NO.3 OUSPENSKY , GURDJIEFF AND FRAGMENTS

Examines the relation between G.I.Gurdjieff and P.D.Ouspensky, drawing on Boris Mouravieff's close friendship with Ouspensky.

ISBN 1-872292-22-4 $9.95 £5.95

NO.4 BELIEFS OF THE PRE-CHRISTIAN SLAVS

Describes the remarkable similarities between the doctrines of the pre-Christian religion of the Slavic peoples, and the classical inner forms of early Christian tradition

ISBN B-872292-22-4 $5.95 £3.95

NO.5 LIBERTY, EQUALITY, FRATERNITY

The famous slogan of the French Revolution and its narrowing effect on world thought, suggesting that a change in the order of words might might actually have given our modern world a different sense of priorities.

ISBN B-872292-23-2 $5.95 £3.95

....

A METHOD OF PRAYER FOR MODERN TIMES
by Eugraph Kovalevsky

A lucid manual for methods of prayer used by the Russian Church - in a form once given by the author to prayer groups in the French Orthodox church and hence admirably suited to contemporary Western seekers.

ISBN 1-872292-18-6 PB $19.95 £13.95

A new translation reveals the spiritual science
of the early fathers.

THE TRIADS OF
ST. GREGORY PALAMAS

Introduction by the Translator, Praxis Director Robin Amis

This unique book, Saint Gregory Palamas' Triads, is of great philosophical, spiritual and historical importance. It deals with the difference between spiritual and scientific knowledge; the Christian enlightenment; prayer of the heart, and the method of circular attention; describing the Transfiguration as a type of true charismatic experience and early ideas of how the Age to Come can be reached in this life.

ISBN 1-872292-15-1 160PP PB $19.95 £14.95

by P.D.Ouspensky
THE COSMOLOGY OF MAN'S
POSSIBLE EVOLUTION

Published with the help of his senior pupils, the only publication of the second series of O's lectures, introducing the important cosmological aspect of his personal teaching.
COSMOLOGICAL LECTURES PB ISBN 1-872292-01-1 £14.95
WITH PSYCHOLOGICAL LECTURES HC ISBN 1-872292-00-3 £24.95

by Boris Mouravieff
GNOSIS - STUDY AND COMMENTARIES ON
THE ESOTERIC TRADITION OF EASTERN ORTHODOXY

An ancient Christian spiritual tradition illuminates the inner spiritual doctrines of the early church. These three volumes address the meaning of human life and history, and its relation to divine purpose and cosmic processes. Boris Mouravieff's Gnosis provides practical information on the development of the heart and the transformation of spiritual energies.
VOL.I EXOTERIC CYCLE ISBN 1-872292-10-0 296 P PB
٠ VOL.II MESOTERIC CYCLE, ISBN 1-872292-11-9 304 P PB
VOL.III ESOTERIC CYCLE, ISBN 1-872292-12-7 304 P PB EACH
$37.50 £24.95 $89.95 £69.95 THE SET

PRAXIS INSTITUTE PRESS
A DIVISION OF PRAXIS RESEARCH INSTITUTE, INC. A NON-PROFIT CORPORATION REGISTERED IN THE STATE OF MASSACHUSETTS

Web-page at www.praxisresearch.org - mail to

Three Barns, Aish Lane, South Brent, Devon. UK TQ10 9JF -

or: 2931 W. Belmont Ave. Chicago, IL 60618 USA

24hr US voicemail (847) 459-1990

e-Mail sales enquiries www.praxis.press@praxisresearch.org

Institute Information www.praxis.institute@praxisresearch.org